Lines of Flight

lines of flight

Reading Deleuze
with
Hardy,
 Gissing,
  Conrad,
   Woolf

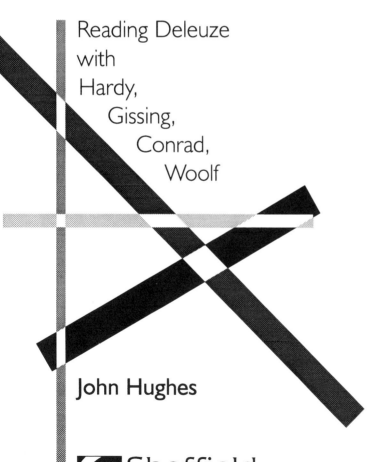

John Hughes

Sheffield
Academic Press

Published by Sheffield Academic Press Ltd
Mansion House
19 Kingfield Road
Sheffield S11 9AS
England

Printed on acid-free paper in Great Britain
by The Cromwell Press
Melksham, Wiltshire

British Library Cataloguing in Publication Data

A catalogue record for this book is available
from the British Library

ISBN 1-85075-807-7

Contents

Acknowledgments

I would like to thank all the present and former colleagues at the Cheltenham and Gloucester College of Higher Education who have helped in numerous ways towards the completing of this book: Philip Martin, Martin Aske and Simon Barker for their kind and practical support, and in particular, Manzu Islam, Sarah Wood and Alan Brown for their more tangible help in reading and commenting on earlier drafts. I would also like to thank friends in other institutions who have either read or offered me the chance to read extracts. These include Michael Carrington, Clare Hanson, Philip Shaw and Roger Ebbatson. Mark Ford and David Hughes have throughout provided invaluable sources of stimulus for a book they have yet to read. Finally, I would like to dedicate the book to Joanna.

Introduction

This book's recurrent contention is that the conception of
ethics that animates Deleuze's work provides literary studies
with productive ways of thinking about the kinds of unconscious activity expressed and elicited by literary texts. The
book, accordingly, is something of a hybrid, as its structure and
ways of working demonstrate. It is an attempt to articulate or
associate an account of the questions of the limits of representation raised recurrently in Deleuze's work, on the one hand,
with readings of various fictions from the Anglo-American
tradition which Deleuze valued for its experimental qualities,
on the other. If, for Deleuze, famously, the thought and activity of which an individual is capable exceed and contest the
integral identities formed by consciousness and the organism,
so also, in relation to a literary text, it is possible to attempt to
read with a primary interest in the affects that the text can
produce and stage, and only relatively in terms of the representations that it makes available to the consciousness that
aspires to speculative comprehension. When Deleuze says, *pace*
Spinoza, that 'there are many things in the body that you do
not know' and 'in the soul many things which go beyond your
consciousness',[1] he intimates that the ethical design is this
concern to think of life in terms of becomings, not representations, with what passes between bodies and transforms them in
their multiple kinds of association. That is, to think in terms
at best of a scrupulous pragmatic inventiveness no longer re-
ducible to the volitional repertoire of choices which is, for
Deleuze, the resource of the fiction of transcendence fostered
by consciousness.

Consciousness becomes rethought, accordingly, in Deleuze's
work as a register of the identity effects that are produced by
the becomings of body and soul as externally related through

their encounters with other bodies and other minds, and no longer thought of as the comprehensive source of individual development, knowledge or freedom. In its political dimension, for Deleuze, following Spinoza, Nietzsche and Bergson, such an idea of ethics involves always a critique of the socially underwritten mystifications by which consciousness is granted a false and impossible priority. However necessary such a mystification is for the derivation and control of moral subjects, then, it nonetheless distorts the innate possibilities of thought because it removes it from its true origins alongside the multiple, unconscious working of the body, and hence from its capacities for autonomy.

In these ways, Deleuze's empiricism contests the privilege assigned to a philosophical image of mind as integrated subjectivity within this contested conception, the functioning of thought is seen to depend on the conjoined working of the mind's various faculties so as to secure in the identifiable and representable object an analogue for the subject's own assumed transcendental identity. The stakes of such an image are high for Deleuze, since it provides a kind of template for an analogically related series of images of order, identity and organization whose conservative linkages and assumptions of mastery define a contrary politics of resistance and change, a nomadic thought. Brian Massumi glosses the political stakes of Deleuze's metaphysics here:

> The subject, its concepts, and the 'external' objects to which the concepts are applied have a shared, internal essence: the self-resemblance at the basis of identity. Representational thought is analogical; its concern is to establish a basis between these symmetrically structured domains. The faculty of judgement serves as the police force of analogy, assuring that each of the three terms is honestly itself, and that the proper correspondences obtain...
> 'Nomad thought' does not lodge itself in the edifice of an ordered interiority; it moves freely in an element of exteriority. It does not repose on identity; it rides difference. It does not respect the artificial division between the three domains of representation, subject, concept and being; it replaces restrictive analogy with a conductivity that knows no bounds. The concepts it creates do not merely reflect the eternal form of a legislating subject, but

are defined by a communicable force...Rather than reflecting the world, they are immersed in a changing state of things...[2]

In a sense, everything which follows in this book is implied in these first paragraphs. The first two chapters provide an elaboration of the philosophical lineage and preoccupations of Deleuze's work as will be most useful for the four chapters on the novels which follow. Inevitably strategic and selective as these expository chapters are, it is further hoped that they will, nonetheless, in themselves and in their interleaving with the discussion as a whole provide some measure of introduction to Deleuze's work. As this suggests, I have imagined a reader with little prior knowledge of Deleuze's work, and so have tried to avoid being overly cryptic or allusive, while trying also to avoid simplification.

It may be, still, that such an account, and all it carries with it of a critical vocabulary that trades in such ideas as the critique of interiority and representation, and the engendering of different potentials of thought and activity and feeling, sounds initially either impossibly utopian, dangerously anti-rational, or romantic, in the first place, or impossibly philosophical, or schematic, in the second. So, for instance, Colin Gordon cites a forceful criticism by Perry Anderson of the possible implications of the valorization of the unconscious productions of desire which the reflections of *Anti-Oedipus* constantly reiterate. These are criticisms which go to the heart of many issues in Deleuze's work:

> The catch-word of desire has...been one of the slogans of the subjectivist *Schwärmerei* that followed disillusionment with the social revolt of 1968—celebrated in such writings as...Deleuze and Guattari's *Anti-Oedipus*, the expression of a dejected post-lapsarian anarchism. Intellectually, the category operates for the exercise of any fantasy freed from the responsibility of cognitive controls...Politically, the notion of desire can lead with the greatest facility to hoary reaction and superstition... their possibility is inscribed in the metaphysical vacancy of the term itself—which can legitimate the desire for death and destruction, just as much as the desire for life and liberty, as its origins in Nietzsche make clear...[3]

For Deleuze and Guattari, the concept of desiring-production works as a means of overturning the idea of the unconscious as a regressive and imaginary realm of interiority, and of recapturing for an activity and description of thought its truly creative unconscious features, and its immanent social relationality. It is true that there is in Deleuze's work, nonetheless, a central Nietzschean emphasis on 'active destruction',[4] and it is as well to discuss this very briefly here, so as to indicate in an introductory way the cogency of Deleuze's notion of desire, and its resistance to the terms of Anderson's criticism. For Deleuze's Nietzsche, 'active destruction' is conceived as a necessary condition for the qualitative change of forces from the reactive to the active, occasioning affirmation by way of a willed negation of reactive forces. To anticipate briefly here a later discussion: if the reactive is what denatures the active by turning it against itself, then the culmination and transmutation of the reactive occurs in its turning against *itself*. So it destroys itself in a destruction now become active and futural, and no longer orientated towards the conservation of its own powers of denial. In this way, the idea of 'active destruction' functions not as the 'legitimation' of nihilism, but conversely as its willed culmination and transmutation. The aim here is to suggest that such a moment of desire has its place within a complex ethical and metaphysical framework in which the dynamic compoundings of forces produce and reproduce their different relative qualities in a crucial aspect by virtue of the necessity of dissociative or destructive moments. More fundamentally, it is important to emphasize also that desire for Deleuze is preeminently a concept which is not identifiable with pleasure or mere spontaneity, but with experimental practice and production as expressions of the compositional and collective potentials of the bodies concerned:

> Do you realize how simple a desire is? Sleeping is a desire. Walking is a desire. Listening to music...or writing, are desires... Desire never needs interpreting, it is it which experiments...They say to us that we are returning to an old cult of pleasures...And above all, it is objected that by releasing desire from lack and law, the only thing we have to refer to is a state of nature, a desire which would be natural and spontaneous reality. We say quite the opposite: *desire only exists when assembled or machined*. You cannot grasp or conceive of a desire outside a determinate assemblage, on a plane which is not pre-existent but

which must itself be constructed. All that is important is that each group or individual should construct the plane of immanence on which they lead their life and carry on their business...[5]

Or as Gordon puts it,

Desire is the fact that mechanisms move, that assemblages function, that virtualities, even those of sleep, are realised, rather than unrealised... A desire is a practice. Desire is a relation of effectuation, not of satisfaction...[6]

The question remains, though, as to how such concepts can be put to work as modes of engaging with, for instance, Hardy or Gissing. Deleuze himself commented suggestively on how English and American fiction can be seen as animated by a distinctive kind of philosophical activity, one which uses language to explore kinds of thought involved in the body, and at odds with the apparent masteries of representation:

English or American literature is a process of experimentation. They have killed interpretation...[7]

Reciprocally, as one can imagine, such experimentation draws the empiricist philosopher into ways of working and writing that can be identified with the novelist:

empiricism is like the English novel. It is a case of philosophizing as a novelist, of being a novelist in philosophy... Empiricists are not theoreticians, they are experimenters: they never interpret, they have no principles...[8]

In what ways might readings of Hardy or Woolf (to take two of Deleuze's own examples) benefit from being considered in terms of such experimental features? In the case of Hardy, for instance, Deleuze has emphasized the 'strange respect for the individual' which we find within Hardy's novels, where 'individual' as a term is differentiated from 'personality' with the latter's recognizable traits and assumed self-identity.[9] The 'individual' here is, broadly, a term for the expression of a self conceived as essentially open to transformation through the accidents of its encounters. Transformation is something that necessarily takes place between bodies. That this is primarily a matter of physicality is borne out in Deleuze's further comment (admittedly somewhat counter-intuitive on the face of it) that Hardy's characters exist, accordingly, as 'a collection, a packet, a bloc of variable sensations…',[10] or, as Tess would have it, 'sheafs of susceptibilities'.[11]

Further, and to anticipate elements of the chapter on *Jude the Obscure*, one could demonstrate how Hardy's narrator employs a language which draws on a suitable power of expressive materiality and syntactic disarticulation, a resistance to the terminus of meaning. This conveys the inimitably Hardyan portrayal of characters involved themselves always in movement, diversity, and an uncertain self-variation. They are undone by inconvenient sympathies or antipathies, or transported by desire. Their experience is diversified by the power or ironies of the moment into fugitive impressions, or superficial, incidental, emotional truancies—by turns tragic in their working out, or comically inconsequential. If such writing can be described as involving a philosophical activity in the sense employed by Deleuze above, then, it is because it makes writing itself a matter of becomings. It works through kinds of experimental activity conceived as upsetting an image of thought as committed to representation, and as offering new powers of individuation to the reader. Writing here seeks to become adequate to the thought involved with the inimitable experimental activity of the body, and to the production of distinctive affects. Accordingly, the individual chapters on *Jude the Obscure, The Odd Women, The Shadow-Line*, and *The Voyage Out* trace the ways these texts elude or surpass in various ways what one can crudely call the generic controls of nineteenth-century fiction. In both expression and content the texts are dedicated to generating in writing hitherto unforeseen potentials of thought and affectivity.

If such a description can justify a book-length study it is because Deleuze's work allows for ways of describing and explicating these features in terms of a distinctive ethics of reading which brings out their real and effective philosophical dimensions, where philosophy is not a matter of providing representations, but something more pragmatic:

> Writing is very simple. Either it is a way of reterritorializing oneself, conforming to a code of dominant utterances, to a territory

of established states of things...Or else, on the other hand, it is a becoming...[12]

It is doubtful that things are as clear cut as this either/or indicates, but it can be said that there is a particularly effective engagement with these questions in the literature of the turn of the century, and its emphasis on dislocations of many kinds. Rather differently, however, it could be said that in these novels a feature, perhaps the innermost one, of nineteenth-century fiction attains at the end of the century its fullest expression. Who, after all, is more importantly a figure of Victorian writing than the orphan, the subject without memory, family, territory, the living reproach to a society which denied him or her prescribed routes of personal development and political association? What takes place in *Jude the Obscure* or *The Odd Women*, perhaps, is an interrogation of those, as it were, official controls and values by which nineteenth-century fictional consciousness sought both to express the fascinations and to control the fears attendant upon movement, and imaged in the packs of urchins who patrolled the urban streets. Retrospective narrative, normative social stratifications, the developmental logic of characterization, the hypostatized uses of point of view—these powers of a strategically artificial production of an image of the real are thrown aside in these turn of the century texts. In so doing it may be that these texts rediscover powers of becoming that refer us back further to what Deleuze conceives of as the novel's earliest history:

> Everything which becomes is a pure line which ceases to represent whatever it may be. It is sometimes said that the novel reached its culminating point when it adopted an anti-hero as a character: an absurd, strange and disorientated creature who wanders about continually, deaf and blind. But this is the substance of the novel: from Beckett to Chrétien de Troyes, from Lawrence back to Lancelot, passing through the whole history of the English and American novel. Chrétien de Troyes constantly traced the line of the wandering knights who sleep on horseback, supported by their lance and stirrups, who no longer know their name or destination...[13]

Finally, if the preceding discussion has indicated various points of affiliation between Deleuze's work and that of other continental thinkers such Derrida, de Man and Lyotard, it is important to emphasize, for reasons that will become more clear, that his work cannot be identified with perhaps more familiar post-structuralist and deconstructive work, and its fixation on the scrupulous delineation of textual aporias. This is in large part because Deleuze's work is highly individual in its influences. In his early monographs on Hume, Bergson, Nietzsche and Spinoza, Deleuze precipitated from their work formulations of ideas of becoming and self-differentiation which in their working out were to offer him the means whereby a critique of a transcendently ordered scheme of things can combine with an affirmative ethics of the immanent. In this connection, Michael Hardt has emphasized how Deleuze's work can be seen as a reiteration and unfolding of the positive ontological and ethical resources offered to him by such philosophers. These he always admired as constituting a kind of minor philosophical tradition, one possessing importantly oblique and critical kinds of relation to the main one:

> I liked writers who seemed to be part of the history of philosophy, but who escaped from it in one respect, or altogether: Lucretius, Spinoza, Hume, Nietzsche, Bergson... All these thinkers are of a fragile constitution, and yet shot through with an insurmountable life. They proceed only through positive and affirmative force...[14]

Something similar surfaced in his own antipathy to the institutionalization of philosophy, and the seminal figures which it coopted in his own education:

> At the Liberation we were still strangely stuck in the history of philosophy. We simply plunged into a scholasticism worse than that of the Middle Ages. Fortunately there was Sartre. Sartre was our Outside, he was really the breath of fresh air from the backyard...
>
> The history of philosophy has always been the agent of power in philosophy, and even in thought. It has played the represser's role... A formidable school of intimidation which manufactures specialists in thought...An image of thought called philosophy has been formed historically and it effectively stops people from thinking. Philosophy's relation with the State is not solely due to the fact that recently most philosophers have been 'public professors'... The relationship goes further back. For thought borrows

its properly philosophical image from the state as beautiful, sub-stantial or subjective interiority...[15]

The strength of Hardt's book is the cogency with which he demonstrates how much of the complex texture of Deleuze's work is woven from the work of these figures, and I shall return to the detail of his account in the next chapter.[16]

1 |

Deleuze and Empiricism

In the last chapter of *Proust and Signs,* as elsewhere, Deleuze describes thought as an encounter with what is essentially outside thought, and which forces it to act:

> ...impressions which force us to look, encounters which force us to interpret, expressions which force us to think...[1]

Thought begins with something which does violence to the expectations and self-possession of consciousness. A kind of paradigm of such an encounter is when its object produces a problem for recognition, as, simply, when a sensation signals to memory since it seems to belong to two places, two times at once; or when the loved one's words signal to the jealous intelligence because they seem to betray a contrary truth. The encounter in such cases is an accident, but this very contingency is seen as the condition in which the creative function of thought is shocked involuntarily into working to rediscover its own necessity as a reading of nuances, signs. Deleuze's empiricism is evident here in so far as thought is constrained to act by sensibility, and discovers the condition of its own creative activity outside itself, and through time: the provocative signs of bodily encounters demand translation in terms of a truth to be discerned. So, the intelligence cannot avoid the discomfiting and unignorable summons of, for instance, a word, a glance, a gesture, or an impression which seems, unsought, to convey paradoxical intimations of complicated senses. The sign thus causes the mind to pass from sensation to the distinctive kind of workings of memory or the imagination which it provokes, and to an engagement with the problem with which it confronts thought. The person who is thinking is drawn, accordingly, into an essentially involuntary, discordant and solitary process of adjustment, in an attempted explication of the repertoire of ideal relations which make up the meaning involved within the sign. (In *Proust and Signs*, Deleuze suggestively likens this labour to the effort of translation demanded by a reader whose deciphering intelligence pursues the meaning that is concealed within the sensible surface of a hieroglyph.)

Without a prescribed path, Deleuze's thinker begins in this way in the obscurity of an enforced response to a problem, not with the beneficent dissemination of a pre-existing and elucidated signification. If it is necessarily something problematic that oppresses and generates thought, as this suggests, this is in an important part because it is a question of the subject's discriminating between available interpretations of the multiple senses of the sign. However, it is also because the mind, in so doing, is inescapably divided between the activities and limitations of its own different capacities, and caught up by what passes between them as it pursues its truth across their different stations:

> The sensuous sign does us violence: it mobilizes the memory, it
> sets the soul in motion; but the soul in its turn excites thought,
> transmits to it the constraint of the sensibility, forces it to con-
> ceive essence, as the only thing which must be conceived...[2]

It as well here to try and unpack some of the implications of this quotation as it bears on the discussion here of Proust. The empiricist response to a sign bears on an essence or an Idea which is implicated within the sign, but which resists representation where representation assumes the synthesis of the perceived and the understood, a presentation which exemplifies the concept. An Idea is a power of determination and differentiation which repeats itself in various guises without being given by any single case which expresses it. In a formulation we shall return to, it is both distinct and obscure, infinitely variable, insistent within sensations and memories which cannot ever adequately present it. Further, it traverses the various faculties of the thinking subject, between which it establishes, as Timothy S. Murphy puts it, a ' "discordant accord" ' (Kant's phrase remotivated by Deleuze) and 'communicates only the violence of its difference from one faculty to another'.[3] So, the mind, in coming across these problematic instances which defeat mere recognition, is put to work in a discordant way.

Thought, along with or instead of other faculties—memory, imagination, perception, sensation—is activated in what is, importantly, a multiple range of potentials, relays, and linkages, which, nonetheless, does not entail a unified subjectivity. If, again, in many places Deleuze describes recognition as the image of thought to be contested, it is because such an image presupposes, conversely, that this multiplicity of mind can be subdued under the rubric of a consciousness which, by ordering the convergence of this multiplicity in relation to a recognized object, accordingly rehearses its own transcendent status. Recognition, then, is in the first place an image of subjective convergence or communication, of a harmony of the different faculties in relation to their commonly conceived object.

Against this, then, Proust offers Deleuze a different case of how thought works:

> No one has insisted more than Proust on the following point: that the truth is produced...that it is extracted from our impressions, hewn out of our life, delivered in a work. This is why Proust rejects so forcefully the state of a truth which is not produced... and the state of a thought which would presuppose itself by putting intelligence 'before', uniting all one's faculties in a voluntary use corresponding to discovery or to creation...[4]

So with Marcel's madeleine soaked in tea, whose flavour animates memory and thought:

> I had continued to savour the taste of the madeleine while I tried to draw into my consciousness whatever it was that it recalled to me...[5]

The little cake works as a sign because it is a problem which provokes a question, and confronts the narrator with the perplexing being of the sensation itself, and with its summons in this case as releasing an affect of joy which goes so far as to seem to make death immaterial. The cake cannot be simply an object of recognition because the narrator finds the essence of the encounter beyond the memories of Combray and his aunt which are soon evoked. Thought is moved here via sensation and memory to a meditation on the essence of Combray itself. This is an essence conceived as an insistent virtuality that repeats itself through the very differences of its actual states, and the multiple kinds of experience it occasions—Combray as both ideal and yet real, though non-existent, a repetitive essence, a virtual being, which signals to thought through the linked yet disjoined instances of a sensory quality, and memory. As the encounter works between and goes beyond sensation and memory, so it confronts each of these with the limit of their exercise, activating interpretation as a confrontation with discordant kinds of material—the sensed, the remembered, the conceived—which cannot be collected into the unified forms of a perception or a memory in recognition. The encounter with the madeleine, or later the paving-stones, bears on the continuity of something ideal which engenders this discordant unity of interpretation, and which signals through and subsists in these divergent moments.

So, on Deleuze's reading, art for Proust is the unfolding of such labours of thought within a stylistic medium adequate to the deciphering of the essence which is folded within a sensible sign:

> ...if thought has the power to explicate the sign, to develop it in an Idea, this is because the Idea is already there in the sign, in the enveloped and involuted state, in the obscure state of what forces us to think...[6]

Thought finds itself outside itself, working from the sensible to essence which operates reciprocally to determine 'the objects which express it',[7] and to individualize the artistic subject who finds his vocation in interpretation:

> truth—and life too—can be attained by us only when, by comparing a quality common to two sensations, we succeed in extracting their common essence and in reuniting them to each other, liberated from the contingencies of time, within a metaphor. Had not nature herself...placed me on the path of art...she who, often, had allowed me to become aware of the beauty of one thing only in another thing, of the beauty, for instance, of noon at Combray in the sound of its bells...?[8]

Essence, writes Deleuze, is the 'quality of an original world', which repeats itself differently through the distinctive relations that are established within and between its varying objects, and whose qualities it raises to a new power of expressiveness. It is identifiable with a new viewpoint that makes of language a style capable of capturing and revealing these common features of a differently conceived and felt universe.

Accordingly, a style is conceived here as a power of meta-morphosis or metaphor, in which two objects 'exchange their determinations', to be seen differently through what is produced through their association as common to them.[9] The ultimate reference of style is, further, not to its material linguistic substance, but to the virtual perspective that is indissociable from it, incarnated within it as a power of differential repetition. Words and things are wrested from their customarily conceived conditions so as to be worked within 'chosen artistic conditions' as the expressions of a new way of experiencing the world.[10] Style is the means of production of a new kind of optical or philosophical effect.

Empiricism is evident in this literary art in various ways. First, it is by means of sensory experience, its qualities and forces, that the persona of the writing is initiated into his task of raising to artistic expression the possibilities of thought and feeling, the unique universe which summons him and whose signs he works to interpret. Second, the writing defines this vocation as an articulation of the qualities that are extracted from the relations of bodies and terms, where these relations function as a kind of exchange and alteration in the outside— the hawthorn lane and Gilberte. A common relation, then, redefines these terms by virtue of a common quality extracted from the event of their paradoxical kind of conjunction. In the third place, the empiricist task as a thinking of relations is repeated not only in the content but also in the form of writing, as the text works to transmit to the reader new affects and qualities of thought. Writing itself becomes a matter of becoming, an aesthetic composition which incarnates through sensation affects which reiterate and make actual virtual potentials of relation. In this way, the reader is drawn into the implicit and hitherto unimagined community which the text anticipates through its matter of expression. And so style reveals itself, finally, in such ways, as a means of individualization which extends to the reader, and which is not identified with the author, since it is only in the process of writing so conceived that the subject position which it conditions is constituted: 'Had not nature herself...placed me on the path of art...she who, often, had allowed me to become aware of the beauty of one thing only in another thing?'

Empiricism so understood, as experimental, whether in philosophy or literature, construes thought, then, as an activity before it is a reflection, an unconscious affect and auto-constructive thought from which empirical consciousness is produced. This is an emphasis that relates Deleuze's last published book to his first, *Empiricism and Subjectivity*, in which he wrote that 'Philosophy must constitute itself as a theory of what we are doing, not as a theory of what there is'.[11] If this so, it is because, as Deleuze continues, '[w]hat we do has its principles'.[12] Or, as Nick Land puts it, '[t]hought is a function of the real, something that matter can do'.[13] Being and thought are the two sides of the creative real, parallel manifestations of a transcendental unconscious. In the terms of *Capitalism and Schizophrenia* they are the means of a machinic desiring production amenable to the critical reflective work of what Land calls a

> Schizoanalysis [which] methodically dismantles everything in Kant's thinking that serves to align function with the transcendence of the autonomous subject, reconstructing critique by replacing the syntheses of personality with syntheses of the impersonal consciousness...[14]

Within the terms of the discussion so far, but in ways which obviously demand a fuller exposition, the subject emerges as a provisional unity, a function of the anonymous and productive multiplicity which the unconscious is. The constitutive affects of body and mind are pre-personal intensities whose qualities depend on differences in magnitude between the forces of the body and those of the bodies it encounters. The affect is a change of state, an increase or decrease in the mind-body's power of action and response. It is related to the affection where the concept of an affection involves a reference of a state of a body to the bodies to which it is related. Thus Brian Massumi talks of how an affection refers to 'an encounter between the affected body and a second, affecting body (with body taken in the broadest possible sense to include "mental" or ideal bodies)'.[15]

So, to return to the case of Proust above, an unconscious affect was construed as a sign by the artist, which is to say that an intensity produced in the encounter with the sign became a problem for a thought constituted outside itself. The artistic faculty and vocation, transcendent though it may be, discovered its own principles in thinking of and from affects whose nature and quality the writer sought not merely to elucidate, but to reproduce within the reader. Style was seen to become a machine for reproducing such processes of unconscious feeling and thought within the reader, while also articulating for consciousness, within the substance of art itself, the virtual viewpoint which they express. Transformed and transmitted through the medium of literature, it was the raising of a response to problems to the level of consciousness which largely forced and defined the becoming of the artist.

Nonetheless, there are, of course, important distinctions as well as connections to be drawn between such an empiricist practice in art, and an empiricist practice in philosophy or science—the three aspects of thought which Deleuze and Guattari identify in *What is Philosophy?* as the means of formation of the human subject:

> At present we are relying only on a very general hypothesis: from sentences or their equivalent, philosophy extracts *concepts* (which must not be confused with general or abstract ideas), whereas science extracts *prospects* (propositions that must not be confused with judgements), and art extracts *percepts and affects* (which must not be confused with perceptions or feelings). In each case language is tested and used in incomparable ways— but in ways that do not define the differences between disciplines without also constituting their perpetual inbreeding.[16]

That is, it is Deleuze and Guattari's aim to interrogate the real conditions of conceiving, observing, and feeling or perceiving, and to account for their mixtures. As Ian Buchanan puts it:

> Philosophy, art and science are humankind's three affects; its three distinguished perceptions; its natural history rendered philosophically.[17]

Each of these aspects is seen in *What is Philosophy?* as a creative struggle of thought with its outside, the chaos of pure immanence, where thought finds itself in the attempt to draw a consistent mode of encounter, a repeatable power of becoming, out of its confrontation with 'chaos as undifferentiated abyss or ocean of dissemblance'.[18] If a concept, or a percept or affect, is not to be confused with discursive or representative instances, or lived perceptions or affections, it is because it presupposes this outside, as an absolute horizon of immanence. It is from this that habits and creations of thought actively emerge through the production of a relative section or plane of consistent immanence, in which are found the transcendental conditions for the events of conceiving or feeling, where each is both a physical and an ideal expression of a possible world. It is to this excessive chaos that the kinds of compositions of philosophy or art are related as autonomous constructions—constructions of the different possible universes to which the sensations and affects of art summon the viewer or reader; constructions of the different 'image of Thought-Being' whose virtuality insists as an infinite potential of variation in the uses of the concept.[19]

A fuller discussion of many of these notions—such as the virtual and the plane of immanence—will follow, but the important emphasis here is that these aspects of thought, in this way, are seen as matters of creative practice. They are what is *done* by philosophy, art and science, as these constitute consistent events and diagrams of physical and mental relation on their plane of immanence. From the purely unformed immanence to which they are related, each discipline of thought creates distinctive, but constantly intersecting and interfering, expressions of potential, possible and actual worlds. So, although each pertains in principle or *de jure* to a different condition of thought, yet there are points of undecidability between them. What they have in common, however, as creative activities is a coterminous rejection of ready-made and conventional clichés and opinions of representation, of the constraints of a thinking which is bound to the repetition of the same as the form of identity.

So also for the philosopher, say Deleuze and Guattari, the problem exceeds the pragmatic and representative solutions it determines:

> All concepts are connected to problems without which they would have no meaning and which can themselves only be isolated or understood as their solution emerges.[20]

As these interconnecting comments suggest, the problem or its equivalents is an important idea in much of Deleuze's work. The problem works in ways resistant to the generalities and subjective concords of recognition, where this assumes a function of explicit communication of understood truths proceeding from the interiority of a subject. The example of poetry as a problematic object for the philosophy of art might provide a way of connecting up some of the threads here. A poem, for instance, could be said to envelop a potentially inexhaustible power of affectivity and meaning, and to engender many different lines and levels of reading. In this way it defines the reader as a kind of open and transformative multiplicity of responses and capacities. But, more than this, a poem can be said to be in itself inimitable, 'a singularity without concept'.[21] As such, its condition of working is found in the power of differential repetition which it both disguises and expresses through its reiterable singularity, and through the actual events of its reading. That is to say, a poem has an ideal dimension which insists through the intrinsically disjoined elements of a forced response. Further, it is this dimension that both determines the variations of interpretation, as pertaining to the poem's describable qualities and designations, while also transcending these as a power of ideal reiteration always repeated as different, and so never presented in itself, and so never a unified object of knowledge or understanding. A poem so conceived is an intensity, a simulacrum, in so far as it is always different from itself, constituted in the form of a paradox which dissolves the identity of a recognizable meaning into the disparities of complicated and divergent readings. It is in such terms that Deleuze writes of Mallarmé's *Book* in *Difference and Repetition* in a discussion which ends by broadening its terms to find in the paradoxes of the simulacrum a means of thinking of the real conditions of becoming in self-difference:

> Everything has become simulacrum, for by simulacrum we should not understand a simple imitation but rather the act by which the very idea of a model or privileged position is challenged and overturned. The simulacrum is the instance which includes a difference within itself, such as (at least) two divergent series on which it plays, all resemblance abolished so that one can no longer point to the existence of an original and a

copy. It is in this direction that we must look for the conditions, not of possible experience, but of real experience (selection, repetition, etc.). It is here that we find the lived reality of a sub-representative domain.[22]

To continue with the example of the poem for a moment, the problematic aspect of a poem is evident, then, as its resistance to ultimate totalizing capture by the kinds of knowledge that it nonetheless elicits. In this way our relation to it is defined as one of learning or discovery, as long as this learning is conceived of as a function of our inability in a real sense to comprehend the poem in itself. The poem is a problem, irreducibly so, and as such essentially inflicts a kind of violence or surprise on the reader, defining his or her relation to it as an affect, an intensity or an action before its meanings are resolved into the reflective and interim, partial, captures of knowledge. In its singularity, the poem works as an event whose problematic status is that its singularity is the disguised expression of a virtual power of differential repetition within the event itself, and which scatters itself across, and subsists within, the divergent operations of the mind and of the body which the poem conditions. In such ways, then, although the poem is not ultimately graspable by the determinations of knowledge, this does not preclude ways of conceiving of its problematic status.

One can accordingly account here for the different values of interpretation as the term is employed by Deleuze, as in *Nietzsche and Philosophy* and *Proust and Signs*, where it refers positively to the discriminating movement of thought towards the Idea under the affective and sensible constraint of the sign. Or, as against this, its negative use in *Dialogues*, for example, as a term which seeks the closures of recognition, of a repetition which would be merely that of the same, of the representations of the concept, or, in that text also, of the Oedipal situation as the theoretically inescapable and general form of psychic experience. More broadly, the following passage from *Difference and Repetition* allows for an important restatement of the main points of the discussion here, as well as a statement of some points that need to be brought out more:

> Problems have an objective value, while Ideas in some sense
> have an object. 'Problematic' does not mean only a particularly
> important species of subjective acts, but a dimension of objec-
> tivity as such which is occupied by these acts. An object outside
> experience can be represented only in problematic form; this
> does not mean that Ideas have no real object, but that problems
> *qua* problems are the real objects of Ideas. The object of an Idea,
> Kant reminds us, is neither fiction nor hypothesis nor object of
> reason: it is an object which can be neither given, nor known,
> but must be represented without being able to be directly deter-
> mined.[23]

That is to say, Ideas and problems are both immanent and
transcendent to the describable state of affairs that actualize
them. So, the representations of the problem refer to something that is in itself undetermined, and that exceeds its
actualizations since these express an Idea. The true exercise of
reading, then, is to confront its problematic limits. This involves a sense of language, to borrow a formulation from *Difference and Repetition*, as both distinct and obscure. Distinct, in so
far as the relations between words and the play of representable meanings between, and as it were, behind them can be
articulated; and obscure because such an activity of articulation bears on an object that is, in principle, problematic and
unknowable. In this way reading moves in an ideal and dif-
ferentiating element, and finds its inventive condition in this
problematic excess. It is in the problematic, then, as the transcendental element of interpretation, that reading finds itself
referred 'to a para-sense which determines only the communication between disjointed faculties'.[24]

Finally, it is important here to emphasize explicitly the practical and productive aspects of this empiricist relation of
thought to problems. Learning is the process by which we
wrest from our encounters not only representations (or alter-
natively, a confounding experience of perplexities), but also
habitual solutions, ways of negotiating and coping with the inexhaustible ideality of the problems that recur in the events of
the singularities that transmit them. The solution functions not
only as a speculative reduction of the activity of learning, a
necessary means of providing it with knowledge, but also as
the production of a capacity which manifests ways of feeling,

sensing and acting, as well as potentials of meaning:

> To learn is to enter into the universal of the relations which con-
> stitute the Idea, and into their corresponding singularities. The
> idea of the sea, for example, as Leibniz showed, is a system of
> liaisons or differential relations between particulars and singu-
> larities corresponding to the degree of variations among these
> relations—the totality of the system being incarnated in the real
> movement of the waves. To learn to swim is to conjugate the
> distinctive points of our bodies with the singular points of the
> objective Idea in order to form a problematic field. This conju-
> gation determines for us a threshold of consciousness at which
> our real acts are adjusted to our perceptions of the real relations,
> thereby providing a solution to the problems. Moreover, problem-
> atic Ideas are precisely the ultimate elements of nature and the
> subliminal objects of little perceptions. As a result, 'learning'
> always takes place in and through the unconscious, thereby
> establishing the bond of a profound complicity between nature
> and mind.[25]

In line with the above, the empiricist tradition that Deleuze's
work seeks to reactivate and renew is dedicated to 'analysing
the states of things, in such a way that non-preexistent concepts
can be extracted from them...'[26] Again, in *What is Philosophy?*,
written with Guattari, philosophy is defined as just this, 'the art
of forming, inventing and fabricating concepts'.[27] It is a creative
thinking that presupposes an essential relation with the
unthought, and whose aim, to cite the Preface to *Dialogues*
again, is 'to find the conditions under which something new is
produced *(creativeness)*...'[28] And what would be produced
would come from a new activity of thought, one involved in
the complex relations of bodies, and propelled towards a new
articulation of these relations. This account of thought contests,
as has been suggested above, rationalist accounts which would
describe experience in terms of the prior dictations or constitu-
tions of subjectivity, and which would assume a controlling
'"common sense"—[a] harmony of all the faculties of a thinking
being'.[29] So too, it contests the reduction of philosophy to the
determinations or paradigms of truthful representation. As Ian
Buchanan has written:

> Rather than investigate the nature of the being of a subject, what
> Deleuze and Guattari want to do is elucidate its becoming.[30]

Accordingly, empiricism for Deleuze entails, as Parnet has memorably said in a formulation which neatly draws together the threads of this discussion, a thought which would 'not be closed on recognition, but would open to encounters, and would always be defined as a function of the Outside'.[31] The rest of this chapter aims to develop these ideas with more explicit reference to Deleuze's work on other philosophers, and his work with Guattari, so as to indicate where necessary something of the range and provenance of his work, as well as of its powers of articulation and transformation.

Deleuze Solus—Deleuze and Spinoza, Kant, Nietzsche, and Bergson

The discussion so far has come to the idea that Deleuze's work develops an account of experience which denies the subject any precedence and superposed unity. It emphasises the subject's differentiation into a multiplicity of transcendent functions, functions defined by their immanent relations to elements of being which they alone confront. First, then, the faculties of thought have an essentially divergent exercise as acts of mind existing in parallel to the manifold sensitivities of the body. As this suggests, Deleuze construes consciousness no longer as the privileged source of representation to which all objects of experience are invariably submitted. In his work on Kant, *Kant's Critical Philosophy*, Deleuze develops sharply this theme of the inadequacies of describing experience in terms of the prior dictations of subjectivity.[32] An important area here is his discussion of the Kantian notion of a transcendental plane, and its assumption of the necessary conformity of what is presented to us as Nature with the *a priori* principles by whose syntheses we represent it.[33] From the psychological or empirical ego, Kant is seen to extrapolate the superior instance or supreme fiction of a unifying and unified, self-conscious self as the foundation of the experiential ego, and as the instance which subjects the conformities of the transcendental field of experience to its determinations.[34]

For Deleuze, as I have suggested, consciousness is displaced or subjected within a differently conceived 'transcendental field',[35] one no longer faithful to the Kantian notion of a necessary rapport of nature with the form of objectivity. It is no longer a question here of the submission of the sensible to the dictates of the laws which govern representation, but of the intermissions of encounters which disarticulate the unity of the subject. Deleuze does not deny that the Kantian faculties of representation—memory, sensibility, imagination, perception and so on—have a transcendent function, and relative orders and hierarchies of working, but he denies their priority and their essential concordance. They retain their transcendence, but on empiricist grounds, in that they exercise their singular principles as a kind of thinking or reading of what they encounter, construed as signs, images, words. They are composed out of these physical encounters, as what occasions them in each case, as the condition which forces or stimulates the events of their recreational exercise. If this situation defeats the totalizing work of recognition, it is in part because what provokes memory or sensibility or imagination or thought as such is a material peculiar to it, and hence unassimilable within the centripetal working of recognition; and in part too because there is that in this situation which forces the faculty to a problematic limit, where it encounters what is given to it alone.

To take up the example of sensibility. Sensation is the exterior orientation of the body involved in encounters with what Deleuze and Guattari call 'elements of matter', and in *Bergsonism*, Deleuze describes this as an encounter in which millions of what he calls the 'vibrations or elementary shocks' of matter are contracted into a felt quality, perceived as a kind of sign for the faculty of sensibility, and so given over to duration, memory and spirit.[36] These vibrations open sensibility again to the being of the sensible, and so occasion the contact of bodies and the operation of mind. The activity of sensibility transcends the innumerable shocks which it is heir to, through the synthetic production of qualities, and in being stimulated so to rediscover its own potential. Yet, at the same time, this act of translation is also exceeded by the material. Whereas subjectivity emerges in relation to the rudimentary individuation developed in sensation, there remains always outside sensation, as in the quotation 'not the given but that by which the given is given', the material condition of forces.[37] In *Difference and Repetition*, Deleuze summarizes this state of affairs by stressing that the transcendent principles are fundamentally empirical since they always 'leave outside themselves the elements of their own foundation'.[38]

What Deleuze's work offers, then, in these ways is what can be described as an immanent metaphysics of experience, without appeal to 'a dimension supplementary to the dimensions of the given'.[39] The transcendent principles which he acknowledges within experience are said to arise from within experience and not to precede it, or to impose themselves from without. Deleuze's polemic against rationalism, for instance, is not a polemic against transcendence, but a polemic against socially determined philosophical distortions of transcendent principles which hypostatize the transcendent acts of mind into the universal and unified determinations of a prior and transcendent mind. The implications of such a distinction between subject and mind are far-reaching, and most obviously twofold. On the one hand, the distinction allows us to consider how for Deleuze, and Deleuze and Guattari, the conditions of experience and subjectivity are 'no more individual than personal',[40] but in an important aspect elude recognition, involving what Constantin Boundas has termed

> singularities and events, that is the intensive magnitudes, out of which the human world, with individuals and subjects populating it, must be constituted...[41]

On the other hand, it is Deleuze's great contribution to have indicated and developed what is at stake here, not merely speculatively, but more importantly ethically and politically. His main resources in his early work derived from his encounters with Nietzsche and Spinoza, for whom also it is true, as he remarked in *Difference and Repetition*, that

> ...[t]he conditions of a true critique and a true creation are the same: the destruction of an image of thought which presupposes itself and the genesis of the act of thinking in thought itself...[42]

Central to his uses of these writers is a critique of representative consciousness in line with the above discussions, which opens, more resoundingly than has been apparent so far perhaps, into an affirmative account of the creativity of the mind, and its political capacities, as well as into a critique and polemic against the social fictions which benefit from such a repressive presupposition. The starting point here is an account of Deleuze's discussions of consciousness which goes along different tracks from the previous discussion, but which leads into these areas.

Throughout his life, Deleuze reiterated an emphasis on the derived and reactive nature of consciousness in relation to the affective relation of forces which compose the body as a 'multiple phenomenon'.[43] In this way the active potential and qualities of the body remain in important ways at odds with, and eclipsed by, the reactive and reactionary workings of consciousness. Deleuze often quotes here Spinoza's remark that we do not even know what a body can do. Deleuze draws from Spinoza the idea that body and mind exist in parallel, with no order of priority or causality between them. The body relates to what is outside itself through its affections, experienced first as the images and contact of another body; and the mind deals in its parallel way with the ideas of these affections. By these ideas of bodily contact, then, the interacting bodies are both represented in the mind. Consciousness pertains to this layering of body and mind in a secondary and derivative fashion, in that it deals in the ideas of these ideas, in the interiorization, doubling and reflection of the ideas which are in the mind as, in the first instance, the relation of thought to the exterior, as the mental correlate of bodily affectivity. Consciousness, then, in the first instance, is belated and without genuine activity, since it is fundamentally a recording, to borrow the vocabulary of *Anti-Oedipus*. It is primarily subjection, since it merely redoubles the idea, as I have said, as the idea of the idea, though it attempts to compensate for this situation by an imaginative fiction, culturally endorsed, of its own priority, moral freedom and purposiveness. More than this, though suggested by it, throughout his work Deleuze develops a critique of subjectivity which emphasizes the negative features of consciousness, and its inwardness with dialectical thought, denial and sadness.

This last point is taken up in Deleuze's hugely influential book

on Nietzsche, *Nietzsche and Philosophy*. In this book, a slightly
different vocabulary notwithstanding, Deleuze identifies in
Nietzsche an account of the formation of self-consciousness in
accordance with the working of an overly controlling memory
which interrupts the original affective working of the body
and mind.[44] Whereas the expressiveness of body and mind
demand to act their reactions to what is outside themselves,
and sustain this potential by an activity of forgetting, in the
case of an excessive self-consciousness this is undone and defeated by the formation of the type of what Deleuze calls 'the man
of *ressentiment*', *ressentiment* being characterized by a mind in-
vaded 'by mnemonic traces...'[45] In the schema of *ressentiment,*
the position of (what in the Spinoza book would be called)
consciousness is secured by a disabling of the necessary
forgetfulness of mind and body, and takes affective form as the
depreciation and blaming of the exterior object which can no
longer be encountered, but only represented in consciousness.
Here, memory and subjectivity have taken the place of the out-
ward orientated activity of mind, and consciousness can only
compensate for its own powerlessness, emotional destitution,
and spoiling by more or less consciously hateful projections
directed against the remembered object whose excitations are
conceived of as an affront since they cannot be adequately
engaged with and comprehended. This has been memorably
glossed by Alphonso Lingis:

> Deleuze concludes that the force that originally excludes the
> memory, the representation of a behaviour and of the situation
> that provoked it, is nothing other than the re-presentation, the re-
> enactment of that behaviour. It is when the force of repetition in
> actuality is unrealized that the repetition occurs in representa-
> tion, that is, in memory. The primary unconscious then is not a
> system that repeats because it does not remember, because a
> memory continually forming is continually suppressed, but a
> system that does not remember, that is, does not represent what
> has come to pass in it, because it repeats it... The primary uncon-
> scious is the positive force of a body that closes in upon itself in
> the positive production of its contentment...[46]

Within *Nietzsche and Philosophy,* Deleuze indicates how the
schema of *ressentiment,* with its complex mechanics for the
interruption and internalization of active forces, provides

Nietzsche with the resources not merely for a profound psychology, but also, importantly, for a history of slaves: this is Western History for Nietzsche as the Judaeo-Christian culture of *The Genealogy of Morals*, with its necessities of indebtedness, guilt, conscience, and asceticism. As for Spinoza here, the typology of a resentful consciousness provides similarly the resources for an analysis of the political forms of those compensations which consciousness generates out of its own secondary status. These are compensations secured above all by the guaranteeing fiction of 'a super-sensible world in opposition to this world, the fiction of a God in contradiction to life...'[47] In *Spinoza: Practical Philosophy*, these resources of critique and creativity are made clearly evident in a passage which brings together many of the concerns here, within their true ethical perspective:

> There is, then, a philosophy of 'life' in Spinoza; it consists precisely in denouncing all that separates us from life, all these transcendent values that are turned against life, these values that are tied to the conditions and illusions of consciousness. Life is poisoned by the categories of Good and Evil, of blame and merit, of sin and redemption. What poisons life is hatred, including the hatred that is turned back against oneself in the form of guilt. Spinoza traces, step by step, the dreadful concatenation of sad passions; first, sadness itself, then hatred, aversion, mockery, envy, humility, repentance, self-abasement, shame, regret, anger, vengeance, cruelty... His analysis goes so far that even in hatred and security he is able to find that grain of sadness that suffices to make these the feelings of slaves. The true city offers citizens the love of freedom instead of the hope of rewards or even the security of possessions; for 'it is slaves, not free men, who are given rewards for virtue'. Spinoza is not one of those who think that a sad passion has something good about it. Before Nietzsche, he denounces all the falsifications of life, all the values in the name of which we disparage life...[48]

For Deleuze's Spinoza, the aims and methods of ethics and speculative philosophy exist in parallel, since knowledge is inseparable from the capacity to act freely in accordance with the intrinsic determinations of one's nature, and knowledge is the knowledge of these relations as expressions of Nature and eternity. Freedom here is not a matter of will, but of the automatic expression of an innate potentiality opposed to all the instances which would seek to distort, subject or damage it. Nor is it a matter of morality, since ethics is an analysis of the means by which the body can maximize its affective capacity, and, reciprocally, deliver itself from the reactive world of established moral values, based as these are on culturally invested mirages of higher worlds of the spirit. For Spinoza, there is no route to happiness and knowledge other than to understand the confused, coercive, and depressive conditions and relations in which emotion and consciousness emerge, and the bad faith of the fictions of transcendence by which temporal states preserve their power, and set their seal on human servitude. Happiness or beatitude is a discovery of the eternal and infinite values of the purely immanent dimension of experience. This is a discovery which necessarily involves a demystification of the tyrannies intrinsic to the state, and to fixated emotional states, and coterminous at best with a maximization of the relational and symbiotic potentials of a creative desire. Learning through experimentation is of the essence of life, as it is the condition of the rectification of all that distorts people's understanding, and the production of new kinds of optics, as for Spinoza, who was employed in preparing lenses. In this sense the development of reason is the same as the discovery of the conditions under which we can develop our autonomy vis à vis the practical expression of the innate resources of our own nature. This idea of expressiveness accords with a conception of the eternal in terms of which one can understand the relational potentials of an existent thing, potentials which it expresses ceaselessly in the form of change, as variations do their implicit theme.

Central to this whole discussion is the account of the body that Deleuze develops from Spinoza's work, most notably in his work with Guattari. As Colin Gordon has pointed out, Deleuze and Guattari use a Spinozist account of desire to contest a neo-Lacanian identification of desire with the unconscious construed as a shadow 'theatre' of regression, deprivation, imagery and verbal representation:

> What Deleuze and Guattari contend for their part is that desire, far from being the theatre of negativity, lack and interpretation, signifies a field of immanence, relation and production... The

primitive ontogenetic axes of desire in the child are understood
as first of all not parental but social and metaphysical. The
unconscious is (if one may risk the phrase, not used by the
authors) an 'exchange with nature'...[49]

A body can only be considered in terms of its affective potentials, its powers of relating, and not 'by its form, nor by its
organs and its functions, nor as a substance or a subject...'[50]
Eschewing any anthropological temptation, Deleuze and
Spinoza describe the ultimate features of the body as the unformed elements which compose it, and which enter into the
relations of motion and rest which characterize its formal
features. These relations define what Deleuze calls a body's
'longitude'. Its 'latitude' is the 'set of affects that occupy a
body at each moment...the intensive states of an anonymous
force (force for existing, capacity for being affected)'.[51] The
productions of desire involve, crudely, the body as related to
its outside, in the event of a new ensemble of bodies. To
conceive of the physical composition of desire, this is made up
of the extensive movements and rests undertaken by the bodies
involved, so expressing through experimentation and contact
something of the repertoire of relations inherent in these
bodies. Corresponding to these expressions are the intensities,
the affects, which are the forces of the body expressed through
its movements and clinches. Within the *unchanging changing*
world of Nature, relations and affects compose and rehearse
what could be called, to continue the theatrical metaphor liked
by Deleuze, small dramatic productions which carry everyone
away.

So the experimental resources, and intensive states, of the
body, for Deleuze, following Spinoza, elude description in
terms of the recognizable forms of a conserved and organic
body, or of an identifiable and pre-given subjectivity. The
encounters of bodies compose *haecceities* of singular kinds,
arrangements or productions of desire, ensembles of coexten-
sive and cofunctional particles.[52] In *A Thousand Plateaus*, this is
described in this way:

> There is a mode of individuation very different from that of a
> person, subject, thing or substance. We reserve the name *haecceity*
> for it. A season, a winter, a summer, an hour, a date have a

perfect individuality lacking nothing, even though this individuality is very different from that of a thing or a subject. They are haecceities in the sense that they consist entirely of relations of movement and rest between molecules or particles, capacities to affect or be affected... Tales must contain haecceities that are not simply emplacements, but concrete individuations that have a status of their own and direct the metamorphosis of things and subjects...[53]

Or again, in *Dialogues*:

Hecceities are simply degrees of power which combine, to which correspond a power to affect and be affected, active or passive affects, intensities...[54]

The haecceity is the event of desire conceived according to 'a plane of Consistence',[55] a Spinozist term for a purely immanent dimension distinct from the plane of 'organization' from which it can be distinguished but never dissociated, and which 'always involves forms and their developments, subjects and their formations...'[56] In such haecceities desire, then, is the expression of a productive symbiosis of bodies, and the affective intensities involved. Desire connects heterogeneous bodies within a new assemblage on the plane it sets out, and it therefore creates an individuation which is another word for the singular compositions of the assemblage conceived as an ideal event, one with its own kind of consistency. The haecceity goes beyond the subject which is a molarized and moralized function of spiritual reaction. Our experience is in this sense unconscious before it is subjective. In fact, the subjective is derived from the unconscious as a kind of reading or consumption of the encounter within the substance of thought. This explains the following comment in *Dialogues*:

Far from presupposing a subject, desire cannot be attained except at the point where someone is deprived of the power of saying 'I'. Far from directing itself towards an object, desire can only be reached at the point where someone no longer searches for or grasps an object any more than he grasps himself as subject...[57]

The discussion so far, then, has arrived at the point where can be understood Deleuze's statement that a conception of desire must deal with 'ensemble of affects which circulate and transform themselves within a symbiotic assemblage defined by the co-functioning of its heterogeneous parts...'[58] This section has tried to bring out how Deleuze's empiricism displaces a rationalist conception of the subject as a principle of unity for mind. Against this it emphasizes the mind's multiplicity, as complicated with the unconscious and outwardly oriented, plural, affective relations of the body, in line with Spinoza's proposition that the 'mind does not know itself except in so far as it perceives ideas of the affections of the body'.[59] Consciousness is a belated effect of interiorization, an effect which attempts to disguise this condition of relative powerlessness by fictions of its own transcendence, and freedom, by construing itself, that is, as the remote cause of the actions it undergoes:[60]

> Of course a multiplicity includes focuses of unification, centres of totalization, points of subjectivation, but as factors which can prevent its growth and stop its lines. These factors are in the multiplicity to which they belong, and not the reverse. In a multiplicity what counts are not the terms or the elements, but what there is 'between', the between, a set of relations which are not separable from each other... A line does not go from one point to another, but passes between...[61]

Desire is the expression of the affective physics of bodies, of their constructive and connective functions, of what brings them together, and passes between them. It actualizes, or enacts, an ensemble of virtual relations by way of the bodies it connects on the plane of consistence which it produces. As with the description of sensation earlier, the principles of experience are on the same level as the materials whose functioning they assemble, and on whose assembling they depend for their own expression. Sensation finds its virtuality in its actualization. Its actualization is dependent on its synthetic exchange with the elements from which it is composed, elements which remain outside the principles founded upon them.

Deleuze—Ontology and Practice

At this stage it is necessary to indicate briefly some of the distinctive ontological underpinnings of Deleuze's work, and its crucial emphases on immanence, experimentation and creativity. In the introduction I mentioned how Michael Hardt has indicated in this area, in what is the most supple and accomplished of accounts, an evolution of Deleuze's critical thought through the work on Bergson, Nietzsche and Spinoza.[62] I shall begin here with the briefest overview, drawn from Hardt, before attempting to make the detail more explicit. Hardt points out that where Bergson offers in the movement of duration a positive ontology of differentiation, and efficient causality, Nietzsche allows for an opening of this onto an ethics of affirmation, of differential repetition encompassed by an ethical, selective, doctrine of the being of becoming in the eternal return. Spinoza provides, further, for a transposition and unfolding of these movements into a politics based on joyful practice as a fundamental ethical and ontological principle, actively constitutive of being, and expressive of a politics of natural right. At the heart of Spinoza's work, for Deleuze, is the former's replacement of the idea of freedom as volition with the idea of autonomy as expressivity.[63]

This 'constitutive ontology'[64] can be approached through beginning with Bergson's concept of the *élan vital*, as the process which expresses that 'life is production, creation of differences'.[65] Life is an essential unfolding of being in the diverse forms of the actual:

> Why is differentiation an 'actualization'? Because it presupposes a unity that is dissociated according to the lines of differentiation, but that still shows its subsisting unity and totality in each life. Thus when life is divided into plant and animal, when the animal is divided into instinct and intelligence, each side of the division, each ramification carries the whole with it... Differentiation is always the actualization of a virtuality that persists across its actual divergent lines...[66]

So the actualizations of life maintain a kind of intrinsic reference to a subsistent unity or origin. In *Bergsonism*, Deleuze expounds in his account of Bergson's work this crucial distinction between the virtual and the actual.[67] The virtual is this ideal unity of actual differences, and is discerned in duration through the movement of differentiation itself. Moreover, the virtual is itself self-difference, as this maybe implies. The virtual can only exist itself in actuality through the differing from itself which is its dissociation in matter, and through the expressions of itself in different forms which it produces. Hardt summarizes this neatly, the quotation here beginning with a citation from Deleuze's earlier piece on Bergson:

> 'Differentiation is the movement of a virtuality that is actualizing itself.'
> Bergson sets up, then, two concepts of being. Virtual being is pure, transcendental being in that it is infinite and simple; actualized being is real being in that it is different, qualified, and limited...[68]

This idea of a movement of being suggests the necessity of the concept of duration for Bergson. Duration is the motor of ontology, since the actual as it is created in the passing moments of the present refers, for Bergson, to a virtual unity that is original and past. The ontological relation of virtual and actual becomes temporal; and being and becoming are both distinguished and identified in the dissociation of the virtual in the actual. Hence, Deleuze talks here too of the necessity of the 'virtual coexistence' of past and present.[69]

If the logic of this placing of duration at the heart of this ontology of differentiation may be clear, its working out can also involve some potentially confounding moments. The purpose here, however, is to give a sense of the debts which Deleuze's ontology owes to Bergson. For Deleuze, a purely immanent, efficient causality operates creatively within duration to produce the multiple, qualitatively differing, actualizations of unified, virtual being. It is a necessary feature of being to be productive. The virtual and the actual presuppose each other necessarily, and manifest their reciprocal necessity as a vital movement of differentiation that, in Deleuze's words, 'is never negative but essentially positive and creative'.[70]

In *Nietzsche and Philosophy*, the Bergsonian ontological notions of creativity, positivity, difference and negativity become clearly played out as ethical notions: qualities of willed forces, actual expressions of power or desire. Bergsonian self-differentiation becomes an expression of the forces which are constitutive of the events of qualities of physical states of affairs and bodies. To answer briefly the questions that arise here, given the evident broadening of this discussion and the greater complexities of the ethical drama which is implied, it is necessary to refer to Deleuze's reading of Nietzsche's idea of the eternal

return. What Deleuze discovers in his reading of the eternal
return is a means whereby the being of becoming as a unity of
multiplicity can be an affirmation, an inwardness of what wills
with the intrinsic movement of life as differentiation and becoming.[71] The eternal return as ethical, then, is evident as the
will's participation in, and confirmation of, the values of such a
differential ontology.

In the first place, as an ethical principle, Deleuze construes
the ethics of the eternal return as a practical rule, in a formulation ironically reminiscent of Kant's categorical imperative,
'Whatever you will, will it in such a way that you also will its
eternal return...'[72] The ethical status of this formulation is
linked to the distinction between the negative will which occurs
only once (since to will the return of the negative will is to will
negatively the negative will itself, and hence to cancel it) and
the affirmative will that wills being (as affirmation), and, as
such, can return (since this is to participate in the nature of
being as the unity of difference). In this respect, Deleuze discovers the being of becoming in a reading of the notion of the
eternal return that provides Bergson's ontology of qualitative
multiplicity with a synthetic principle of affirmation constitutive of an ethics of the will to power:

> Eternal return, as a physical doctrine, affirms the being of
> becoming. But, as selective ontology, it affirms this being of
> becoming as the 'self-affirming' of becoming-active...[73]

Finally, the work on Bergson and Nietzsche finds its expansion and recapitulation within the work on Spinoza. As Hardt
writes:

> Spinoza's politics is Bergsonian ontology and Nietzschean ethics
> transported to the field of practice...[74]

For Deleuze, in his two texts on the philosopher, Spinozist
ontology has as its essential resource the speculative notion that
being exists fundamentally for the singular mode in its internal
power to express, through its inmost material productivity, the
principle of creative self-difference common to the whole of
being. Such an affirmative ontological principle must in turn
be related to the corresponding political practice which is
animated by the creative principle attendant upon joyful

passion, as the working through of common notions in terms of political association. The central idea here is this of the common notion as the basis of the creativity of joyful encounters. The common notion is wrested from experience as a representation of the relational compatibility between bodies. The common notion is, accordingly, a practical tool for the discernment of adequate possibilities of fruitful compatibility, common relations, between bodies and for the production of new common bodies. In the process it becomes a way of participating creatively in a rational self-knowledge, which is at one with the self-constituting activity at the heart of being. The importance of the term 'expression' for Deleuze's reading of Spinoza becomes apparent here. The politics implied in such ideas implies the rejection of tyranny and the pursuit of freedom of association as intrinsic to the political realm. Ethics, as will be evident below, demands the rejection of moral norms and the *status quo* in themselves as inhibiting factors of pseudo-transcendence alien to the self-expression of the intrinsic unknown potential of citizens.

In this way the common notion allows for the drawing together of various threads here. As a practical tool of knowledge it presupposes an activity of experimentation and self-transformation, of becoming-other (to anticipate Massumi below). For an interval, customary, even instinctive, identities are unlearned or forgotten in the intensification and selection of other affective potentials within a particular environment shaped by desire. Such a process involves body and mind in concert, in an expressive and autonomous activity which reiterates the virtual scope of the body's affects by a kind of experimental selection from them, one dependent upon the relations that can be actualized, and that can evolve, in the concrete situation, the exterior milieu. Brian Massumi emphasizes the ethical nature of such an activity, as opposed to morality, which he describes as the socialized attempt to segregate thought from the body by recourse to values of its transcendence:

> Becoming-other goes from the general to the singular, returning thought to the body, grasped from the point of view of its transformational potential... It is eminently ethical, in Spinoza's sense of tending towards an augmentation of the power to live in this world...[75]

And what takes place here, to illustrate a point touched on above, can be seen as an individuation which, while involving agency, cannot be simply identified with the form of the person, not least since it is in the commonality of bodies and a process of learning that a larger ethical and political body is anticipated and formed. So too, it is through this commonality that the expressive potential of the individual is actualized.

Deleuze and Guattari—Becoming-Other

The final remarks in the last section are ways of approaching something of the meaning and value that the term 'becoming' takes on for Deleuze and Guattari, as it describes the contact of previously separate bodies. Becomings for Deleuze and Guattari are productions of desire involving at least two terms animated in a movement or rhythm which becomes common to both, as a compounding of their powers of relating. In a sense what is produced can often defeat prediction, not only because it is an actual experience, a singular occurrence and event, but also because it results in a qualitative alteration of both bodies beyond what each has been. Nor does becoming essentially suppose the terms to be involved within a chiasmic exchange of properties, or in kinds of transposition or mimicry. In *Dialogues*, in the following passage, Deleuze very clearly outlines the strange artifices of becoming by recourse to the example of the conjunction, or nuptials as he calls them, of wasp and orchid. The orchid reproduces by way of enticing the wasp into its sexual functioning, and the wasp feeds as it fertilizes the orchid:

> Nuptials are always against nature... The wasp and the orchid provide the example. The orchid seems to form a wasp image, but in fact there is a wasp-becoming of the orchid, an orchid-becoming of the wasp, a double capture since 'what' each becomes changes no less than 'that which' it becomes. The wasp becomes part of the orchid's reproductive apparatus at the same time as the orchid becomes the sexual organ of the wasp. One and the same becoming, a single bloc...'an a-parallel evolution...'[76]

In terms of becoming, the dialogue between wasp and orchid is a pragmatic and imaginative suspension of the separable and habitual status of the bodies involved, and of those pre-given, predictable and conditioned responses which constitute what appear to be their integral identities. Instead, they participate in a kind of creative symbiosis, which is made up of the 'a-parallel' combination of their two activities. Although these activities are different in kind, they nonetheless combine to create a new common movement, one which engenders new affects, and which is itself open to further transformations and adaptations. Deleuze and Guattari write of this example also in *A Thousand Plateaus*:

> The line, or the block, does not link the wasp to the orchid, any more than it conjugates or mixes them: it passes between them, carrying them away in a shared proximity in which the discernibility of points disappears...[77]

A kind of confluence emerges between the bodies involved which testifies to kinds of fluctuating bodily potentials merging into the indiscernibilities of the proximity which defines an encounter.

Some of the most influential of Deleuze and Guattari's ideas can be unfolded from such an example: becoming-other, deterritorialization, line of flight, minoritarian becoming, the body without organs, assemblages, among them. To remain for the moment with this wasp and orchid example, the becoming-other in which both wasp and orchid are caught up, as in the last quotation, creates a deterritorialization of each, where each becomes involved in the state of a body not previously or recognizably its own. Each now enters a liminal zone outside of its own territorial and reproductive, organic, functioning and form. Here it can experiment with, and attune itself to, new connections (as if each becomes also a kind of open waveband for tuning processes of the other). This involves an extreme differentiation of bodily potentials, a new kind of multiple and sensitized autonomy in relation to various stimuli inherent in the situation. Massumi again makes the point:

> The body-in-becoming does not simply react to a set of constraints. Instead, it develops a new sensitivity to them, one subtle enough to convert them into opportunities—and to translate the body into an autonomous zone effectively enveloping infinite degrees of freedom. The body is abstracted, not in the sense that

> it is made to coincide with a general idea, but in a way that
> makes it a singularity, so monstrously hyperdifferentiated that it
> holds within its virtual geography an entire population of a kind
> unknown in the actual world...[78]

Outside the interiorizing, molarizing, orbits of customary
thoughts and organic form, the body finds new opportunities
of expression. Its unconscious participation in the outside converts into a kind of flight and unforeseen self-expression, as the
body's functioning is raised to a new and creative power in the
event of the new affective commonality in which it is constitutive. The unconscious here is, of course, both physical and
mental, an affective conjoining of the body; and, for thought,
an attuning to signs and signals.

The line of flight is a concept that encompasses these moments and senses, and many others, of this power of becoming.
It involves a deterritorialization through a movement which
interrupts or suspends familiar, confining, formal possibilities
and their prescribed organic and social requirements. Such a
flight is seen by Deleuze and Guattari not as an escape from
reality so much as a production of and engagement with it, a
movement out in which the participating bodies are drawn
along new vectors in experimental ways. And through this con-
juncture or common movement, new qualities are taken on by
each. This is another way of conceiving of a thought of the
outside, beyond recognition. This would be an experimental
thought of the body, an empiricist creativity, untimely in the
many senses of Nietzsche's phrase, and abstract in the ways
that Deleuze indicated in an interview:

> The notion of the abstract is a very complex one: a line may
> represent nothing, be purely geometrical, and yet not be purely
> abstract as long as it still traces the contour of something. The
> abstract line is the line which doesn't mark a contour *of*
> anything, but instead passes *between* things—a mutant line. In
> this sense the abstract line isn't a geometrical line at all, but the
> most living and creative of lines. Real abstraction is a non-
> organic life. The idea of non-organic life is constant in *Mille
> Plateaux*, since it is the life of the concept...[79]

Further, the body for Deleuze and Guattari contains multitudes. This is true in at least two main senses that require more

explication. First, in the sense that in the process of becoming the body becomes a kind of virtual cloud, an unactualized multiplicity of potential intensities dependent on the body's powers of sensitivity. And so its potential for condensation or distillation will depend not only on these, but on the conditions offered by what it encounters. Or, to vary the metaphor, like a wave, a body will actualize its potentials in ways that depend on the sympathetic or antipathetic channels, or currents or resonances, available in the encounters and milieu immediately open to it. So then, again, the unconscious thought of the body works through the encounter with another body to read the signs which can provoke a new affect, the event of a new becoming unidentifiable with its current form or identity. Deleuze in the following example himself describes the unconscious in terms of the geographical rather than the historical, so as to emphasize that what is important here is this sense of a physicality, of a repertoire of sensitivities, as the condition of what we think of as personality. And so again, the intention is to offset notions of autonomous careers of the spirit, of the self as a principle of transcendence, of monolinear development, and molar integrity:

> At each moment we are made up of lines which are variable at each instant, which may be combined in different ways, packets of lines, longitudes and latitudes, tropics and meridians, etc. There are no monofluxes. The analysis of the unconscious should be a geography rather than a history. Which lines appear blocked, moribund, closed-in, dead-ended, falling to a black hole or exhausted, which others are active or lively, which allow something to escape and draw us along?[80]

Second, and equally importantly, the body contains multitudes in the connected sense that in the process of becoming the body participates necessarily in a new political grouping, perhaps as yet shadowy or odd in conception: a social multiplicity in becoming that is inherently revolutionary and unrecognized. This idea is developed most famously by Deleuze and Guattari in their book on Kafka, where they explore how, even for a solitary individual, this unconscious participation within a counter-society, a new collective, a new conjoining of bodies can be taking place, defining an important part of what they refer to as a 'minoritarian-becoming'.

Finally, this leads into an area that can seem to be at once one of the most forbidding and the most simple in Deleuze and Guattari's work, but which has already been touched on throughout the discussion so far: the 'body without organs'. It is a concept that is perhaps best approached through its necessity within a description of the immanent working of desire as a power of constructive association and transformation. Desire, as it has been described above, requires that the body expresses itself through encounters which exceed the hitherto acknowledged functions of its organic and subjective character. The body without organs is the pure matter, the given type of substance, of which such desire is made up and which expresses it. Desire arranges and composes a plane of consistence where its new connections or syntheses can be assembled, its new constructs be put together. The body without organs in this way is the field of exteriority presupposed by this conception of desire:

> It seemed to us that desire was a process and that it unrolled a plane of consistence, a field of immanence, a 'body without organs', as Artaud put it, criss-crossed by particles and fluxes which break free from objects and subjects... Desire is therefore not internal to a subject, any more than it tends towards an object: it is strictly immanent to a plane which it does not preexist, to a plane which must be constructed...[81]

So, to conclude this section, for Deleuze and Guattari, the encounter of bodies on a purely material level depends on a certain common deforming of their organic or subjective limits. The encounter is reconstrued in more fluid and diversified terms, according to the logic of a pre-personal plane of immanence which provides a means of thinking of the affects which are produced in the exteriority common to the unformed bodies. No longer conceived in terms of organic possibilities or qualities, these bodies can liberate new expressive potentials in the matter of the plane of consistence. Ultimately, new combinations and forms are wrested from these encounters, which define life here as metamorphosis and experimental learning, as obscure movements of thought and body in the outside. Importantly, these are movements which need a potentially fatal and violent interval of dissociation from what have been organized states, and in which the soul finds itself anew in the recreational construction of new stages, the production of new ensembles.

2 |

Deleuze and Reading

In the previous chapter the idea, and even the activity, of reading were invoked intermittently in passing to suggest their continuity, even inwardness, with the terms of Deleuze's empiricism. As this might indicate, it is not merely that Deleuze's work may offer distinctive ways of reading texts, especially what we think of as literary texts, but that, broadly, empiricism itself can always be thought of as a kind of reading—as an enforced response to the implications of material signs. And conversely, that reading can be thought of as a kind of empiricism—where reading a literary text demands a critical activity in which the reader works towards creating a valid language for the different and untotalizable elements of a text that work on him or her. Accordingly, also, the discussion of Proust indicated how a text elicits the articulation of a distinctive viewpoint on and through itself.

As a kind of initial foray into these areas, both empiricism and literary experience might be said to involve an attitude of readiness or openness which risks a certain disturbance to the preconceptions of self-consciousness or will, so as to enhance and maximize, and surprise into operation, different powers and types of thought and feeling. Both might be said to be caught up in an activity of learning and exploration, and to involve a kind of innate truancy, in relation to the prescriptive and unifying values of consciousness. The sympathetic or antipathetic aspects of the encounter which a text produces lead to different kinds of creative thought, and new affects. What becomes of primary importance here is what a text does, the becomings that it can constitute between itself and the reader.

The literary implications of this schema will be explored in the rest of the book, where the discussions centre on how texts

by Hardy, Gissing, Conrad and Woolf work on the reader.
How, for instance, such fictions intensify effects of suspense,
surprise, disappointment, violence, movement, so as to draw
the reader into a kind of critical passage or interval, what
Deleuze and Guattari denote as a 'zone of indetermination or
indiscernibility', which ultimately eludes the activity of interpretation or recognition.[1] In a sense many of these ideas or emphases have long had a familiar currency with literary critics
and theorists, but it is the aim of these chapters to indicate
something of the particular nuances and originality of Deleuze
and Guattari's work, as well as its many interworking aspects—
ontological, ethical, political, aesthetic, even psychotherapeutic.

More immediately, these literary features are expanded in
the following section of this chapter, which seeks to develop a
sense of how Deleuze and Guattari might affect our ways of
reading. It does this by offering strategically a close reading of
a poem by Whitman, a poet they often refer to in passing. This
discussion radiates out also into an account of certain other
concepts employed by Deleuze and Guattari, and hitherto
more or less unmentioned. The emphases of these literary discussions could be announced by the following extract from *A
Thousand Plateaus*:

> There is no difference between what a book talks about and how
> it is made. Therefore a book also has no object. As an assem-
> blage, a book has only itself, in connection with other assem-
> blages and in relation to other bodies without organs. We will
> never ask what a book means, as signifier or signified; we will
> not look for anything to understand in it. We will ask what it
> functions with, in connection with what other things it does or
> does not transmit intensities, in which other multiplicities its
> own are inserted and metamorphosed, and with what bodies
> without organs it makes its own converge. A book exists only
> through the outside and on the outside...[2]

In the final part of this chapter there is a discussion of these
implications of Deleuze's work in relation to Paul de Man's uses
of the term reading. There are important comparisons here. In
the work of both thinkers the encounter with literary language
is seen to suspend the communicative and representative functions of language, engendering another type of thought which

insists on what is ultimately dysfunctional in the material conditions of these subjective moments. In short, in each case a
kind of unreadability compasses the incompatible possibilities
of reading derived from it. Nonetheless, there are important
distinctions to be drawn, however summarily, between these
typologies of unreadability, and where they come from, philo-
sophically. If such a brief comparison has value here, it is in so
far as it clarifies the kind of intervention which Deleuze's work
can make in the practice and theory of reading literature.

Whitman

The Whitman poem is 'Mother and Babe':

> I see the sleeping babe nestling the breast of its mother
> The sleeping mother and babe—hush'd, I study them long and
> long.[3]

Although so short, this is a poem that can produce a whole
range of affective responses, positive and negative, guarded
and unguarded, and it is interesting how the poem stages these,
and draws the reader into them. Perhaps the most remarkable
effect of the poem in this respect is the way in which it comes
to induce in the reader a particular kind of rapt intentness.
This dissolves the conventional distinctions of identity and self-
possession with which the poem begins, and to which it returns
in a more provisional and equivocal form as it ends. Rhythmically, this unfolding and refolding of consciousness is produced
in a kind of variation or counterpoint which perturbs the
strained iambic features of the first and final phases. That is to
say, there is a kind of unformed indeterminacy of rhythm
which dilates the middle of the poem, most notably announced
by the rhythmically insistent and interruptive word 'nestling'.
As this suggests, this less organized rhythmical movement in the
middle is an expression of the way the poetic 'I' is surprised
into a kind of forgetting of selfhood as he passes into a kind of
inwardness with the affective world of the baby and mother.
The word 'nestling' conveys this surprise and this inwardness
semantically also, since it suggests a kind of telepathic and unconscious involvement with an affective situation that is not
objectively given, and that may defeat expectation, since the

sleeping child is not nestled by the mother, but nestles, transitively, her breast. This expression seems held or suspended between two senses—the child nestling against the breast, or the child nestling the breast as in holding it in a nest. This latter sense suggests a strange rapport here, given also in the internal rhyme of nestling and breast, that draws the poet-onlooker, who is now looking rather than seeing, into kinds of affective circuit which are less straightforwardly compatible with the forms of bodily integrity and preconception.

Through such features of language a new combination or ensemble of bodies occurs, one no longer easily convenable within the scenario of the poem, and deriving from a kind of dissolve of the integral limits and breaks on which self-possession and self-consciousness depend. This is at one with the poem's capacity also to embarrass us through its unguarded nature. It must be emphasized, of course, that the affective interval which is the poem's middle phase is given over to something more apparently sterile at the end of the poem. The participle 'hush'd' is odd for all sorts of syntactic and semantic reasons. Initially it appears to hang—as indeterminately referring to babe, or mother primarily. Nonetheless, we are then forced by the clause that follows the word 'hush'd' to attach it to the 'I' who ends the poem, 'hush'd, I study them long and long'. In this last clause there is a sense of the onlooker's quandary, as he passes, as it were, inside and outside this scene, and seems at the end to have a divided sense of his relation to it. So, on the one hand, the clause 'I study them long and long' marks the assumption of a well-meaning kind of contemplation, but this seems also to hold at bay something in part unconsciously sinister, an envious fascination perhaps, also marked by the word 'study'. In this respect, the onlooker is returned to the demarcations of his conscious adult, and presumably male, self and his separated affective condition. These divergent but incompatible affective responses correspond here to a critical kind of self-division or self-difference. Along the same lines, the repetition of the word 'long' suggests also that the second 'long' may be a verb. This would obviously suggest a longing that has been reawakened by the scene, but whose element remains outside the workings of a consciousness returned ultimately to a predominantly defensive sense of its own powerlessness.

In these ways, the poem remains distinct and obscure at the same time, staging acts of representation that it also exceeds. The speaker's indefinite, interminable 'study' can be seen accordingly as the prolongation of the confrontation of consciousness with the involuntary operations of unconscious desire which the encounter with mother and child elicits. A temporally lost affect is reawakened, perhaps in the speaker's longing for inwardness with mother and baby. But also, perhaps, there is a sense of an effort to bring to consciousness itself also the extent to which desire here at the end of the poem has become 'incapacitated', defined by lack and resentment and the requirements of subjectivity.[4] The richness of the poem is obviously at one with the ways it sustains these and other divergent kinds of reading. In these ways, the poem becomes a literary version of the study of the body's affections which Deleuze celebrates in *Spinoza: Practical Philosophy*:

> The entire *Ethics* is a voyage in immanence; but immanence is the unconscious itself, and the conquest of the unconscious...[5]

What links, then, can be made between this analysis of the poem and the larger purposes of this book? First, it can be said to bear out Deleuze and Guattari's description of a haecceity, quoted in the earlier chapter, as a potential of literature:

> Tales must contain haecceities that are not simply emplacements, but concrete individuations that have a status of their own and direct the metamorphosis of things and subjects...[6]

The haecceity is an event of becoming, of an individuating composition of bodies according to their affects, and not according to their recognizable formal features. The bodies come together, hang together, are collected, in an assemblage of desire which produces a common affective plane and becoming outside of the punctual or stative terms of identity. Individuation takes place between things, preceding, undoing, and producing the individual self according to the expressive potentials of its singular molecular elements as unformed materials co-resonating and communicating within their milieu:

> ...it is the I and the self which are the abstract universals. They must be replaced, but in and by individuation, in the direction of

the individuating factors which consume them and which constitute the fluid world of Dionysus. What cannot be replaced is
individuation itself. Beyond the self and the I we find not the
impersonal but the individual and its factors, individuation and
its fields, individuality and its pre-individual singularities...
That is why the individual in intensity finds its psychic image
neither in the organisation of the self nor in the determination
of species of the I, but rather in the fractured I and the dissolved
self...[7]

In the reading above the poem was said to be divided from its
middle by such an event, and by the kinds of deterritorialization involved whereby woman and babe, and by a kind of
contagion, reader and onlooker, were held together, more or
less involuntarily, in a complex individuation. This is a kind of
intermissive and reversible becoming which in that case pulled
all concerned into a larger movement, and which divided the
poem between a time of states and a more dynamic and affective time of process, between a kind of joy and a kind of depression, as between looking and seeing.

Similarly, and secondly, the poem holds the reader in an
activity of reading divided between recognition and a susceptibility to more fluctuating, free-floating, and paradoxical effects
of language. The words, accordingly, can be seen as signs in the
sense invoked at the beginning of Chapter 1, as objects which
defeat recognition because they have two or more senses at
once, and so prolong the time of reading indefinitely, even
as they condition also its contractions in the translations of
thought. This can be linked to the Deleuze of *The Logic of Sense*,
for whom logic and common sense in reading are both
conditioned and exceeded by a kind of virtual sense. This is a
paradoxical potential which stretches words in two directions
at once, as obviously in the word 'nestling' which transmits a
kind of affective transformation to the form of expression and
the form of content alike. To the form of content, because the
conventionalized distance involved in a generic representation
of mother and child is undone by a word which comes to
mean different, opposed and yet not actually incompatible
things. The word has taken on an expressive materiality which
pulls the onlooker and reader into a degree of participation
within a transitive and paradoxical circulation of affects—the

child becoming-woman, the woman becoming-child, the reader becoming-woman, becoming-child, and so on. The spatial demarcations of seeing are interrupted by the relay of affects as intensities produced by the unconscious participations of bodies within an open and continuous moment. An affective transformation is transmitted to the form of expression because the rhythmical and sonorous features of the poem set up a counterpoint with the word 'nestling' which intensifies the physical displacement of representation within the poem. As in a lullaby, language becomes a means of transmitting physical affects, of inducing unconsciousness and a merging of identities. In these ways, the relative separations of content and expression have themselves becomes scrambled in the poem's raising of language to an expressive materiality, in which the descriptive function of language becomes displaced or possessed by bodily rhythms of association, by vibrations and resonances.

So then, the analysis of the poem has suggested that an iambic pattern was emphatically transformed in the middle of the first line in ways consonant with the disturbance of the onlooker's customary sense of the relations of baby and mother, and of his relations to them. To take this further, in *A Thousand Plateaus*, Deleuze and Guattari assign a singular privilege to the idea of rhythm in relation to such transformations. In 'Of the Refrain', Deleuze and Guattari distinguish what they call the productive repetition of rhythm from the operations of a merely mechanical or reproductive meter which would be once again the return of the same, as the logically identifiable, rather than the insistence of a difference. This is connected to the idea of transcoding (as in the case of the wasp and the orchid), whereby two terms evolve and differentiate themselves by a reciprocal capture and involution of parts of the coded identity of the other. Rhythm is a concept that Deleuze and Guattari use in this context to describe the way in which this double capture is at one with a creative intensity, both terms carried away in a movement of becoming corresponding to a verb of uncertain voice since it is uncertain here what would correspond to the linguistic values of the active and passive. From the interaction of the mother and child is effected a different kind of dynamic and unconscious accord, surpassing where each of them began, or what they could predict or intend. The musical analogy would be with the new plane of counterpoint that is created by two musical phrases, passing between each and holding them together, while elevating them to a new rhythmical power:

> Nature as music. Whenever there is transcoding, we can be sure that there is not simple addition, but the constitution of a new plane, as of a surplus value. A melodic or rhythmic plane, surplus value of passage or bridging...[8]

Deleuze and Guattari and Literature

Minor Literature

In the reading of the poem the literary question soon became not what the text could mean but what it could do: the poem considered then, not simply as a verbal construction but also as a constructive event. Variable and reiterable, always differently readable, the poem is also divided and further divisible on each reading, and plays upon the reader in multiple ways which can be at once inseparable yet incompatible. Such a reading comes to include many diverse things, to exchange different signals with the reader depending on his or her changing and coexisting affections. To return to the encounter of mother and babe and breast in the content of the poem, there is a kind of double capture here which is not merely displayed *within* the poem, incalculable and paradoxical as it is, but which signals to the reader's unconscious, and works on him or her, *reads* him, and pulls him into a new kind of grouping. As, for instance, when the 'I' of the poem seems, at least intermittently, and latterly in a complicated way, to surrender his conscious, even physical, position to a different type of participation.

If, for Deleuze and Guattari, this poem can be identified with the name Whitman, it is, accordingly, not by virtue of what could be identified with a poetic figure or a biographical person. Instead it is by virtue of his being, as it were, the opportunity or medium for a dislocating, transpersonal power of becoming whose mobility is inseparable from its aspirations, its reachings out and forward. The poem becomes the event of a non-personal and multiple voice which passes through, or takes up, the speaker and which summons all concerned into a new assemblage of bodies, a new haecceity. There is a promise of individuality here which is no longer the resource of the personal:

> the proper name brings about an individuation by 'haecceity', not at all by subjectivity... Charlotte Brontë designates a state of the winds more than a person...An assemblage may have been in existence for a long time before it receives its proper name which gives it a special consistence...[9]

Hence the Whitman-effect could be described as an overcoming of subjectivity in an invention of a creative physical passage, a line of flight, flight here to be understood not as renunciation, but as the means for a revitalization of a collective potential:

> The more you create your own regime of signs, the less you will be a person or a subject, the more you will be a 'collective' that meets other collectives, that combines and interconnects with others, reactivating, inventing, bringing to the future, bringing about non-personal individuations...[10]

In political terms these threads come together most forcibly for the study of literature in Deleuze and Guattari's concept of minor literature, developed in *A Thousand Plateaus* and *Kafka: Toward a Minor Literature*. The interiorizing, centripetal tendencies of a major use of language (towards the prescriptive form of a moral and national subject, for instance) are contested by a minoritarian use. In this there is the counter actualization of a further capacity of language which opens the major use to fluctuation, to tendencies or unrehearsed opportunities of political association and transformation. For illustration, Deleuze and Guattari cite a 'constant or standard' form for the major use:

> Let us suppose that the content or standard is the average adult-white-heterosexual-European-male-speaking a standard language... Majority assumes a state of power or domination... whereas the minority is the becoming of everybody, one's potential becoming to the extent that one deviates from the model...[11]

The minoritarian use of language has always an existential urgency in so far as it arises in each case from the particular exclusions and exigencies of writers whose immediate linguistic and cultural, sexual or racial situation is in itself complex and multiple. Such a writer must offer a critique of the major language with its assumptions of appropriate and homogenizing forms, subjects and objects, and announce through their displacement in his or her writing a new kind of virtual collective political subject, a new 'collective assemblage of enunciation'.[12] For Deleuze and Guattari, this is clearly so in the case of writers like Kafka or Joyce, who compound the forces of becoming and diversification which they can draw on from their situation between languages and cultures. Kafka who spoke Yiddish, 'a Czech Jew who wrote in Russian...', or Joyce:

> This is the glory of this sort of minor literature—to be the revolutionary force for all literature. The utilization of English, and of every language in Joyce...operating by exhilaration and over-determination...[he] brings about all sorts of worldwide reterritorializations...[13]

Minor literature works to collapse the edifices of what Reda Bensmaia has called '*a single* national language, *a single* ethnic affiliation, *a single* prefabricated cultural identity...'[14]

Whereas the operations of minor literature can be most directly experienced in the writings of those for whom minority is a political condition or predicament, it will be obvious that its potentials extend to every particular man or woman in so far as they resist being subsumed by the recognizable forms of identity working within a culture, a language, a nation. Minor literature, then, can be seen as answering the broadest kind of imperative:

> How to become a nomad and an immigrant and a gypsy in relation to one's own language?[15]

In this broader application of the concept, minority is a resource of all writers who seek to dislocate or deterritorialize the major language, to overturn its transcendent forms, so as to extract its lines of flight, of becoming:

> he finds his strength in a silent and unknown minority that belongs only to him...he does not mix another language with

his, he shapes and sculpts a foreign language that does not pre-
exist *within* his own language...[16]

The minor writer develops inimitable stylistic features by the
different ways he or she plays on language to pull from it
expressive traits that exceed the functions of representation
or the values of speech. Language itself becomes intensive,
inclusive of as yet unformed potentials. The concept of minor
literature thus becomes a way of talking of a kind of experimental political unconscious as a productive and collective
means of desire in literature. The minor use of literature rein-
troduces it to its plane of immanence, of material disorganization, from where its powers of becoming can be drawn. One
can describe this approximately as the way in which the minor
writer effects a mutual transfer between the forms of expression and content, introducing each to their common zone of
expressive materiality. Where major literature assumes the
dominance of a form of expression over the form of content
which it conserves, in a minor use of literature, content becomes expressive and expression becomes material.[17]

   This discussion of minor literature is best prefaced with some
brief remarks on the uses which Deleuze and Guattari make of
the concepts of expression, matter and content, form and substance which they draw from the linguist Louis Hjelmslev. The
essential point is that expression and content have separate,
distinct forms and materials, and yet suppose each other
functionally, in that expression dominates the form of content.
From this, Deleuze and Guattari derive far-reaching implications and uses beyond the analysis of language solely, and
beyond this discussion.[18] Nonetheless, there are several important preliminary points to emphasize here. The first is that
expression, in so far as it organizes content, remains necessarily
blind to the material potentials of its own ordered substance,
as, for example, when to represent something in words is, *qua*
representation, to eclipse awareness of the shapes and marks on
the page, or the unmeaning physicality of sounds, or the substance of thought itself, depending on the material of expression involved. Secondly, as this might suggest, an expression
is a kind of encounter with a content, and can by itself be
encountered as a form of content in another expression, and

another substance, as when writing becomes read, or then again when this reading is discussed verbally. Thirdly, expression as a selective and organizing function is the means of power. The encounter of forces becomes regulated by a repertoire of expressive possibilities, restrictive forms of expression and content amenable to institutional recognition and reproducible identifications.

In minor literature, then, workings of power are contested in these ways: content becomes expressive; expression becomes material; and the formal controls of major literature become resisted, making of literature something that resists recognition as it releases new intensive forces. For instance, in writing about Beckett, Deleuze discusses how the writer distends and ramifies expression, and hence makes it emphatically inclusive of all kinds of bifurcating, endless, fluid multiplicities of sense. More than this, language itself becomes possessed by its inherent physicality, is placed into movements by sonorous intensities that will not resolve into recognizable meaning. So, where the major use of writing, with its premium on good forms, would subdue such stutterings of syntax, the minor writer, like Beckett, may exploit these to make language partake of something non-linguistic, like an erratic movement of the body:

> It is Beckett who perfected the art of inclusive disjunction; this art no longer chooses but rather affirms the disjointed terms in their distance and, without limiting or excluding one disjunct by means of another, it criss-crosses and runs through the entire gamut of possibilities... It is true that these affirmative disjunctions, more often than not in Beckett, refer to the air and gait of his characters: an indescribable way to walk, by rolling and tossing...[19]

As expression can be seen to take on physical properties usually identified with bodies, so, conversely, deterritorialized, physical elements of language can overrun expression. In broad terms such a transfer is carried out first by playing on the expressive materiality of contents, so letting writing develop from the a-signifying—the purely sonic, in sound, the asyntactical in syntax. Language approximates, in this aspect of its use, to an involuntary animal cry or whoop, as well as unfolding a conductive surface of proliferating multiplicities and becomings

of sense that cannot be simply prescribed, or subdued by interpretation:

> We find confirmation of this in one of Beckett's poems that deals
> specifically with the connections of language and turns stutter-
> ing to the poetic or linguistic strength par excellence...he places
> himself in the middle of the sentence, he makes the sentence
> grow from the middle, adding one particle to another...in order
> to direct the course of a block of a single, expiring gasp... Cre-
> ative stuttering is what makes language grow from the middle,
> like grass; it is what makes language a rhizome instead of a tree,
> what puts language in a state of perpetual disequilibrium...[20]

In these ways, then, words resist the stabilising distinction of
expression and content, and the function of representation.
Writing plays on, and develops from, the expressivity of its unformed materials. To take a further example, in *Kafka: Toward a
Minor Literature* Deleuze and Guattari explore how Kafka's texts
seek to elude the grid-like constraints of a particular representation of the human body as a sedentary, familiar, familial, and
submissive content, whose characteristic physical pose is to be
bowed down, and whose appropriate form of expression is
portraiture. Kafka's texts stage disruptions, deterritorializations
of this state of things, at the level of content, so that rapid
and unforeseen straightenings and movements of the body, as
well as unmeaning sounds and gestures, introduce themselves,
sweeping the character away. In various obvious senses the
character is no longer there as a subject of representation. First,
in the sense that he is physically departed, or outside the frame,
or in movement, or unrecognizable because of the inhuman
distortions or transformations of his gestures or expressions.
Content here becomes expressive without having discovered
an appropriate form of expression. So, as yet, such manifestations of desire are critical of a falsely normative state of things,
and productive and expressive of feelings, but without being
finally readable.[21]

Secondly, the character is no longer a subject of representation in this sense also: he is no longer a subject, and so cannot
be represented within any pre-given political scheme. He has
become different from himself, a party to new individuations,
and so in this aspect resists analysis in terms of personal,

human, adult, familial, male, or even organic identity. The lack of a recognizable means of expression here expressed through an unrecognizable expression becomes, then, a means of political intervention and untimely politics, a means of disruption, in Kafka's texts, of the workings of expression. Further, in *Kafka: Toward a Minor Literature,* Deleuze and Guattari oppose this formalized compositional function of portraiture to experimental uses of language in which its representative status is overthrown by a kind of revolution in its materials of expression. Language is affected by invasively expressive, but unsignifying, manifestations of its sonorous material. This affects both the means and subjects of representation itself. Speech and body both become disrupted by persistent noises, animal sounds, crackings, and so on, by sounds partaking of the purely physical. Sound leads to an 'active disorganization of expression' which reacts on content, the cry prefacing the movement away and out:

> What interests Kafka is a pure and intense sonorous material that is always connected to its own abolition—a deterritorialized musical sound, a cry that escapes signification, composition, song, words—a sonority that ruptures... In sound intensity alone matters... As long as there is form, there is still reterritorialization, even in music...[22]

Sound becomes a means of exceeding the dominating functions of major literature, in ways similar to the Beckett example:

> Thus, through its way of 'taking flight' sound brings into play a new figure of the straightened head that now moves 'head over heels and away'... Thus, we find ourselves not in front of a structural correspondence between two sorts of forms, forms of content and forms of expression, but rather in front of an expression machine capable of disorganizing its own forms, and of disorganizing its own forms of content, in order to liberate pure contents that mix with expressions in a single intense matter. A major, or established, literature follows a vector that goes from content to expression... But a minor, or revolutionary, literature begins by expressing itself and doesn't conceptualize until afterward... Expression must break forms, encourage ruptures...[23]

What appears crucial here, then, is the moment of encounter in literature where the operative and conservative distinction of the form of content and the form of expression is exceeded and forced open. An irruptive intensity of the material of expression, and the expressivity of contents, displaces these distinct co-implicated strata into a fluency of becoming, and defines an inclusive line of flight. Contents are no longer subdued to an oppressive objectification, expression is no longer in the service of a singular enunciative subjectivity. Minor literature, then, could be said to be a form of deconstruction if the term is taken as invoking in untimely fashion the imminent actualization of new collective subjects, hitherto virtual, through a pushing of the language of major literature into a state of emergency, of deterritorialization:

> To make use of the polylingualism of one's own language, to make a minor or intensive use of it, to oppose the oppressed quality of this language to its oppressive quality, to find points of nonculture or underdevelopment, linguistic Third World zones by which a language can escape, an animal enters into things, an assemblage comes into play...[24]

Intermission

This discussion has been made up of various interworking strands, and in the case of minor literature, it is evident how the ontological and ethical conceptions at work in Deleuze's writing are implicit, replayed, in the detail and argumentative trajectory of his writings here with Guattari on the revolutionary political uses of an unformed expressivity in literary language. In such ways, Deleuze's work itself takes on rhizomatic characteristics. That is, it becomes a means of interconnecting, enveloping and associating different argumentative and conceptual strands and levels. One could go further and say that one of the most intriguing aspects of reading Deleuze is the sense that each book *includes* all the others in itself, in potential, and all their apparently diverse subject-matter. So, for example, a reading of *Coldness and Cruelty* will resonate with a reading of *Kant's Critical Philosophy* in ways that are far more subtle and manifold, and important, than may be obvious from any purely discursive analysis of the obvious points of contact and difference between the two books. If Deleuze can and even must repeat himself in every book, it is because perhaps he commits to the page no self that is not open, multiple and changing, constructed out of his encounters with different kinds of philosophical material, a way of working that makes of his encounter with the reader also a powerful, and even liberating, experience. Such a way of working implicitly challenges the category of author, as does the nature of his collaborations with Guattari, and even Foucault, perhaps, or Parnet. The proper name becomes one repetition of an intensity, a virtual power of difference which is explicated more comprehensively the more variations we come across. So, the books resonate with each other to define Deleuze's work as a transformative multiplicity which exemplifies itself through the various masks that it assumes in series—Nietzsche, Lucretius, Spinoza, Kafka, Artaud, Lewis Carroll, Bergson. And so also these are writers who have been denigrated by the history of philosophy to the extent that their work offers powers of experimentation which also refuse the form of authority, and which can neither be accepted nor ignored by that history. So these writers haunt the institutions of philosophy as figures of the outside, making for Deleuze the minor tradition of which he speaks. If, in his monographs and elsewhere, Deleuze has sought to reanimate these figures through the scrupulous concentrations of his expositions, it is because they open thought to powers of becoming-other. Thus, the very literalness and concentration of Deleuze's writings on these figures captures from them once again the resources they offer his thought for an introduction to its unrecognized outside. It is a way of emphasizing those features which disturb the major workings of philosophy itself as an instrument of the recognizable, all those emphases in short once again which philosophy cannot ignore: desire, the body, difference, becoming, the unconscious, and parodoxes and problems.

Further, it is interesting here, as a further aspect of this, to see how such neglected emphases become picked up by Deleuze, in a deconstructive fashion, from within the writings of those who are conventionally seen as the figureheads of the philosophical tradition of representation, as with the work of Kant and Plato. So crucially, in *Kant's Critical Philosophy*, Deleuze opens Kantian transcendental subjectivity to ungrounded and impersonal forces, to a productive and diverse unconscious exorbitant to the logic of recognition. This emerges in the argument, referred to earlier, that the common sense which unifies the faculties in different proportions and hierarchical representative functions must presuppose their free and unregulated activity and syntheses. Once again, Deleuze's writing is a kind of clarifying medium, a powerful reagent, in which denegated emphases and potentials in philosophy are raised to a new clarity and dignity and power. The tradition which has sought, in Deleuze's metaphor, to cage the powers of difference in the interests of resemblance and identity is offset as these powers are released in such ways by Deleuze's writing. In short, the nature of Deleuze's intervention in the history of philosophy exemplifies his recurrent emphasis on the necessity of a critique whose destructive and creative elements are inseparable.

Moreover, the features of Deleuze's work discussed here also exceed the category of reader. It is after all a paradox how the extreme rigour and restraint of Deleuze's prose and argumentation becomes the condition of the power of his work to clarify the reader's affective experience. One does not in principle merely assimilate a paraphrasable content in Deleuze's work, but is affected by it in all sorts of practical ways. It offers a power of individuation as a function perhaps of its own refusal to be identified with the form of personality. If the dangers of such an encounter can be all too apparent, so also the benefits it offers are, nonetheless, enabling and real.

To take one final example which offers a neat coming together of many of the strands here, as well as anticipating the next section, Paul Patton has expressed many of these issues with extreme lucidity. Patton discusses how Deleuze in *Difference and Repetition* draws from Plato an analysis of the simulacrum as an unidentifiable carrier of forces of becoming (both/and; neither/nor), not merely resistant to the Platonic values of identity and similarity, but dismissive of them. Platonism is overturned from within, because the simulacrum threatens the distinction of a thing and its representation. The simulacrum involves within itself both resemblance and difference, but differs from a copy in so far as it aspires not to reproduce the appearance of a thing according to similarity, but to emphasize through similarity its difference from it. Similarity is here an effect of something that will not be subordinated to resemblance, but which repeats its own difference as an effect, or, one might prefer, effects its own difference as a repetition. This ensures its status as both nonrepresentational and affective, seeking 'to transmit states of experience or to produce effects in the viewer'.[25] Patton's comments indicate clearly the ontological and ultimately aesthetic stakes of Deleuze's work, as well as providing a neat summary of many of the issues discussed here:

> To assert the primacy of simulacra is to affirm a world in which difference rather than sameness is the primary relation. In such a world, there are no ultimate foundations or original identities; everything assumes the status of a simulacrum. Things are constituted by virtue of the differential relations which they enter into, both internally and in relation to other things. This is a world of bodies defined only by their differential intensities or powers to affect and be affected, a world of qualitative multiplicities defined only by their powers of transmutation, a world of rhizomatic assemblages and nomadic war-machines. In such a world, the mode of individuation of things would be more akin to that of an electrical signal, understood as that which flashes between differential potentials, or to that of haecceities, understood as a complex configuration of intensities...[26]

In short, this is the world of the eternal return of difference, where there are no original things, no external ontological foundations, and where everything to a lesser or greater degree is constituted only in so far as it repeats itself as different. Identity and sameness are reduced to a secondary functioning. They are the masks of a drama of becoming whose essence is that the nature of things is only transformation and dissimilation, a difference masked in a repetition, a repetition masked in a difference:

> taken in its strict sense, eternal return means that each thing exists only in returning, copy of an infinity of copies which allows neither original nor origin to subsist... When eternal return is the power of (formless) Being, the simulacrum is the true character or form—the 'being' of that which is. When the identity of things dissolves, being escapes to attain univocity, and begins to revolve around the different. That which is or returns has no prior constituted identity: things are reduced to the difference which fragments them, and to all the differences

which are implicated in it and through which they pass...the simulacrum is the sign in so far as the sign interiorises the conditions of its own repetition...[27]

Literature and the Affect

In Chapter 7 of *What is Philosophy?* Deleuze and Guattari undertake a long and difficult meditation on the nature of the expressivity of the material of art (and necessarily this discussion is somewhat pragmatic in its selection of those elements from it which can be of most use here). The writer's words and syntax, the painter's paint, the notes of music: these are once again seen as the means of representation only secondarily. Indeed, again more radically, the function of representation in art, providing the subject with an ancillary domain of objective experience, is contested and displaced for Deleuze and Guattari by an artistic creativity which creates as they see life creating, through the experimental couplings and becomings of the forces which compose the body as a multiple phenomenon.

In particular, the discussion in *What is Philosophy?* stresses the essential relation of art and sensation, in accordance with this emphasis. Art is dedicated to producing and preserving in its substance sensations in their being. But what is meant by sensations, by the emphasis on their being, and what is the nature of the relation of sensation to the substance of art? Finally, what are the implications of Deleuze and Guattari's discussion of literature for the critical readings which follow?[28]

Of central importance here is the activity of sensation as the incorporation of something other, the coupling of diverse terms, in an unformed matter of expression which goes between, and partakes of both since it vibrates or resonates with new movements and consistencies produced between or among these terms, according also to its own expressive potentials—textures, timbre, colour, rhythm. As with the discussion of minor writing above, a minoritarian use of style is, in a crucial aspect, the making of language a means of expression not of communication, a means of access to new powers. If this is so, it is in so far as the material of language can work as a conductor of sensations or intensities which 'summons forth', on the far side of a deconstituted subjectivity, narrative, and knowledge, 'a people to come', announced through making the standard or major language 'stammer, tremble, cry, or even sing'.[29] More broadly, then, such an art has not to do essentially with memory, perception, affection, as such, but with the preservation in its material of possible passages, encounters, between things. Art is a resource for syntheses of body and thought which proceed outside of identity, and reiterate an eternal power of becoming in the production of ever new expressions of relating. These passages elude once again the forms of the human, and the repressive aspects of the cultural and social traditions of identification by which these forms are conserved in their recognizability. The matter of art is the means of sensation as the constitution of becoming:

> The affect is...man's nonhuman becoming... Andre Dhotel knew how to place his characters in strange plant-becomings, becoming tree or aster: this is not the transformation of one into the other, he says, but something passing from one to the other. This something can be specified only as sensation. It is a zone of indetermination, of indiscernibility, as if things, beasts and persons (Ahab and Moby Dick, Penthesilea and the bitch) endlessly reach that point that immediately precedes their natural differentiation. This is called an affect. In *Pierre; or, The Ambiguities*, Pierre reaches the zone in which he can no longer distinguish himself from his half-sister, Isabelle, and he becomes woman. Life alone creates such zones where living beings whirl around, and only art can reach and penetrate them in its enterprise of co-creation. This is because from the moment that the material passes into sensation, as in a Rodin sculpture, art lives on these zones of indetermination...[30]

In line with this it can still be said that art is a continuation of life by other means. However, this is so only if art is understood once again in terms of a production of affects in which, as here, the body is effectively disorganized, undifferentiated. This would be as in a picture in which the face is momentarily given over to an animal or childhood quality which deforms its developmental history, and expresses the incorporeal event of a pure affect as a strange symbiosis, a quality of becoming-child or becoming-animal that unseats and eclipses self-identity. If this is in a sense, as lived experience, only momentary, it is also as sensation an expression of the eternal in Spinoza's sense beyond its material manifestation. This is in so far as the sensation expresses the 'internal agreement' of the essences of the bodies involved as expressions of eternal, affective truths of bodily activity as external relation.[31]

In this example of the painting or photograph, the pure affect here has a virtual aspect which cannot be reduced to the real passion which is undergone by either a person depicted, or the viewer or painter. The picture's true status is as a virtual event which conjoins singular elements as the idea of a quality or power of becoming which is expressed in the picture. The pictured body expresses a new complex compound of unpredictable forces, a pure affect, in the ways the particular material features of the body and medium allow. In this way, the artwork actualizes a dissolve of forms and the emergence of a new individuation—an animal- or child- or plant- or woman-becoming, it may be—whose power of metamorphosis summons also the viewer. In these ways, personal identity and history and the norms or conventions of painting are obscured, or eclipsed, here, for the artist (though equally so for the person he or she paints, or the person who views the painting) by affects which have this power of individuation and dissolution. Nonetheless, as indicated, these affects are themselves neither individuated nor undifferentiated, because they are not actual affections, but insistent, virtual compounds of potentials of relating and becoming which are incarnated in the matter of art, but never exhausted by it. As a virtual event the art work is always renewable, variously reiterable, in its effects as an ideal composition expressed on the canvas or in the photograph. Art in these ways aspires to be the 'monument' of an affect, incarnating in its matter of expression ideal potentials of relationality. So, the artwork takes on the status of an event of the virtual expressed through its matter as a reiterable potential of relations exceeding any states of affairs that is depicted. The affect becomes sensible in the matter of expression, releasing contents into new expressive individuations. As an event, the art work reiterates the potentialities which insist within its sensible material. In its virtual aspect as effecting incorporeal transformations, then,

> The monument does not actualize the virtual event but incorporates or embodies it...life higher than the 'lived'...[32]

Art, then, is seen in ways which repeat some of the ideas discussed earlier, as an incorporation in a sensible material of a reiterable event of becoming which draws into its affective interval the compounding of the forces of the unconscious with the forces of an encountered outside. What are important are the immediate effects of a material which signals to the one who views, or the one whose affective becomings are otherwise introduced into the painting, only in terms of tendencies, forces, and ideal lines of becoming. And so too, the material signals change. It provokes fear or desire in the ones who are involuntarily drawn into it, and constituted by it as no longer viewers or readers. To talk of subjectivity here is to talk once again of a subjectivity become plural and multiple, experimental and unformed, an affair of pre-individual intensities, a function of the synthetic and unconscious thought of the body. These are the actualizations expressive of the virtual affect incorporated in the material of art.

How, though, more exactly do Deleuze and Guattari describe the detail of how sensation is at work in art? The work of art preserves a being of sensation as 'a compound of percepts and affects' independent, it has been said, of the lived perceptions and affections of the artist or his or her viewer or reader. Once again, not the perception, that which one sees, but the percept as the virtual event of a becoming by which newly constituted relations of things and self are given to be seen. Similarly, not the affection as a transitory state of feeling, or the affect as a transition itself merely, but the affect as a reference to the virtuality that insists in the partings and combinations of pre-individual elements and intensities which exist as what is expressed, given to feeling. Not the perceived or the felt, but that by which what is perceived or felt is perceived or felt, to paraphrase again. In this way the affect and the percept exceed states of affairs to capture the adventitious time of becoming, the interval of pure suspended possibility. This is the unconscious activity once again of body and thought, defining art itself in terms of an essential experimental function. Sensations take on being, and are held in an artistic composition which transcends its material support, even as this remains their condition and primary reference. The material of art is the means for other things to have another life as they are expressed in it, not represented by it. Their powers of affecting are realized for sensation through the work on the material, so that art becomes physical, preserving the composition of bodies which releases the particular affect. Such a composition is a monument of their eternal potentials caught in this arrangement:

> Sensation is not realized in the material without the material passing completely into the sensation, into the percept or affect. All the material becomes expressive...[33]

Art celebrates and preserves an eternal potential of becoming-other. Not the resemblance of a thing, but an affect of it, then, preserved in a material which becomes expressive of it. The affect of paint becomes a sign in the sensation of a becoming of that which has passed into the material. And so too the artist is swept up, in a double capture which is the real action of creativity. For the writer, Deleuze and Guattari describe a becoming-other in the percept released in words as the action of a landscape which summons character or reader into a different assemblage of affects, or haecceity. Beyond understanding or preconception, the percept is an event of a becoming-landscape which signals and captures us:

> The novel often rises to the percept—not perception of the moor in Hardy but the moor as percept; oceanic percepts in Melville; urban percepts, or those of the mirror in Virginia Woolf. The landscape *sees.* Generally speaking, what great writer has not been able to create these beings of sensation, which preserve in themselves the hour of a day, a moment's degree of warmth (Faulkner's hills, Tolstoy's or Chekhov's steppes)? The percept is the landscape before man, in the absence of man... This is true of all the arts: what strange becomings unleash music across its 'melodic landscapes' and its 'rhythmic characters', as Messiaen says, by combining the molecular and the cosmic, stars, atoms, and birds in the same being of sensation? What terror haunts Van Gogh's head, caught in a becoming-sunflower? In each case style is needed—the writer's syntax, the musician's modes and rhythms, the painter's lines and colours—to raise lived perceptions to the percept and lived affections to the affect...[34]

The material is raised to a different power of expression by what is expressed through it; and what is expressed through it changes equally because of this unformed relation with the material. In modern painting, for instance, the material is promoted in all the singularity of its textures, tones, and their local combinations, at the expense of form as a representational function involving the removed viewpoint of a viewer. The aesthetic plane of composition is subject to a deterritorialization which makes the art work an affair of affects, not of consciousness. Again, of modern literature and music:

> It is characteristic of modern literature for words and syntax to rise up into the plane of composition and hollow it out rather than carry out the operation of putting into perspective. It is also characteristic of modern music to relinquish projection and the perspectives that impose pitch, temperament, and chromatism, so as to give the sonorous plane a singular thickness to which very diverse elements bear witness...[35]

In terms of fiction, Deleuze and Guattari see it as the task of the novelist to generate effects of movement out of the elements that he or she combines in a state of material tension, to dismantle representation as a constraining work of identifiable meaning, so that the text hangs together as a provisional composition always open and in process. As in the discussion of the poem above, a text carries within itself material resources, of language and the elements it conjoins—mother, babe, onlooker—by which reading is maintained as an activity resistant to paraphrase, and in which the reader is drawn by the text into surprising ways of relating. This could be described as the process by which in that poem the reader is drawn out of himself or herself in ways that are by turns attractive and threatening. In this respect the reader can be said to be *read* by the poem paradoxically, as was said, in that the experience of reading is an activity of learning, dependent on the poem as a kind of machine whose effect is to read the reader. So, in reading 'Mother and Babe', one explores one's unconscious potentials of feeling, so as to learn, maybe against one's will, of sympathies or antipathies that surprise and disarticulate one's sense of identity and self-consciousness. In a sense, this defines a further dimension of the poem's complexity, since the studying of mother and child in the poem is equally for the speaker a studying of the ways in which his encounter with them involves an interminable self-reading. This is a learning whose rigour and inclusiveness is a condition of the poet's creative confrontation with problematic features of his own work, as well as of our complex relation to the work.

This emphasis on the way literary texts involvedeterritorializing movements of language and identity and form will be a recurrent, if often implicit, emphasis in the discussions of fiction in the main part of this book. The uses of Deleuze and Guattari for these discussions are that they provide a range of ways of investigating how the texts studied exemplify obscure voyages of the spirit (often tragic in fact) that go beyond standardizing and recognizable forms of narration, experience and community. In these late nineteenth- and early twentieth-century fictions, language and drama can become adequate to intervals of becoming whose essence is at once loss, as well as the untimely anticipation of hitherto unthought potentials of individuation. Of course, these now familiar ideas of critique and creativity as resources of an ethical thought must be employed with caution. So it will be necessary to look at the complexities and nuances, and ambiguities, of their involvement within these fictions with the more static and hierarchical values of identity, narrative and meaning which they seek to displace. In various ways, these texts could be said to respond to a question as to how a text can be put in motion, so that their inventive movements also encompass the reader in conjunctions that constantly surprise or shock.

To recapitulate briefly, then, the affect emerges as a non-organic power of becoming in which the body is caught up, and such becomings are what art seeks to preserve and perpetuate, for Deleuze and Guattari, and make available perpetually. The body is written or painted not in terms of a reference to a character or a figure, nor in terms of narrative, history, personality, or psychology primarily, but through the artist's working of a material to capture and transmit, and explore, sensation itself, the unfelt sources of feeling, the unperceived sources of perception. Representation is turned upside down, and everyone, artist, viewer and subject, is worked on by the art work. They are sympathetically or antipathetically drawn into the compounding of forces which the work seeks to bring towards expression through its material, so that the material becomes what passes between and which makes things pass outside themselves in their own materiality. So, if stone, sound, colour, paint, words can be said to intensify effects of dissonance, purity, rhythm, timbre, ambivalence, this is their essential function (if it could never be their single one, since there can never *not* be reterritorialization also). It is a function which includes the viewer or reader or listener as an element of expression, outside him or herself, within the compound of sensation as it were. This power of becoming depends, then, as existence, on the material, as of paint or stone, for instance, and its durability. But in so far as it refers to the subsisting of an eternal repetition of difference, it is not identical with this durability, this duration. Art aspires to combinations which express affects as qualities of power whose ideal essence can neither be separated from nor identified with the facts of such combinations. Before or beneath the conscious subjectivity involved in reading, there are diverse, unformed, pre-individual and plural joys and diminishments within language.

Deleuze and Guattari's account of art may nonetheless appear in many ways an affront to common sense and general opinion, extreme and provocative even to literary theorists used to credos about the incompatibilities of representation and its physical means, and the celebration of the body. However, if this is so, their view is consistent, as has been stressed, with the broadest ranging philosophical or ethical analysis of thought as primarily an unconscious exploratory activity, coexisting with the body as an unformed potential finding its expressivity in the outside. For them thought aspires to the creation of concepts as pragmatic delineations of bodily relations, and deals with the ideal problems incarnated in the diversity of such encounters. It is fed on problems and paradoxes, becomes by them. These emphases about art become also a way in which Deleuze and Guattari's writing can itself transmit intensities, and become through the strange dispassionate rigour of their expositions, an affect, a new kind of deterritorializing force and transformative intervention within art history, aesthetics, or literary criticism.

Reading: Gilles Deleuze and Paul de Man

De Man

If Deleuze's work allows for such a positive intervention in current literary theoretical discussion of the nature of reading, this is, perhaps, not merely in so far as he is an empiricist, but in that his empiricist emphasis on the externality of relations determines his linguistics as a pragmatics. To bring out the distinctiveness of this, this discussion sketches some points of departure of his work from that of Paul de Man, taken as a figure whose bringing together of literary and philosophical issues has also many points of contact. This is also to gloss more clearly the literary theoretical orientation of the discussions which follow.

From Deleuze's work, as from Paul de Man's, an account of reading can be drawn out whose potential is inseparable from a pronounced sense of the critical status of the encounter with literary language. So then, to anticipate the ways an account of reading can be drawn from Deleuze's work, how might one describe or summarize the differences between this and de Man's account? Certainly, it is necessary in doing this to discuss their different types of intellectual provenance, and the ways in which the discrepancies of language and representation are put across in each case, and I will return to some of these points at the end.

Initially, however, it is important to stress the different kinds of affective tonality in their work. If, for de Man, famously, reading is structured as an aporia, a predicament, an impasse, this is to mark its aspirations to representation, and the problematic pathos of the endlessly reiterated undoing of this aspiration. Deconstruction, for de Man, traces the ascetic narrative of the endlessly displacing oscillation which prolongs reading between the inseparable and divided textual levels of the rhetorical and the cognitive: image or persuasion; and concept. Literary language determines reading as the reiterated discrepancy of a cognitive necessity with a treacherous rhetorical condition. More or less implicit in de Man's work, and his uses of the idea of reading, is a critical situation in representation which forces another kind of thought beyond that of recognition or understanding. However, this remains an imperative internal to the textual activity of reading from which it derives, as the self-divided remarking of an aporia. If Deleuze's empiricism offers the possibility of a different literary theoretical idea of reading which would not be enthralled by undecidability, it may be in part because the undecidable from the viewpoint of recognition or understanding is not seen as the outcome of reading so much as its starting point. Reading begins with problems, signs which force thought by acting upon the body. Moreover, language is pre-eminently, for Deleuze and Guattari, not a means of representation, but a pragmatic tool employed in the interests of a society by anonymous and impersonal 'collective assemblages'. It is a tool for the controlling of bodies and the defining of subjects and knowledge in relation to the exigencies of circumstances. It is 'made not to be believed but to be obeyed, and to compel obedience...'[36] Language acts upon bodies by implicitly transmitting a command that they assume non-corporeal, ideal, attributes. Language conveys convictions rather than seeking to convince one might say, with the literal example in mind of the sentencing, the incorporeal transformation, by which a judge, as the mouthpiece of a larger collective body, makes a convict of the accused:

> In effect, what takes place beforehand (the crime of which someone is accused), and what takes place after (the carrying out of the penalty), are action-passions affecting bodies (the body of the property, the body of the victim, the body of the convict, the body of the prison); but the transformation of the accused into a convict is a pure instantaneous act of incorporeal attribute that is the expressed of the judge's sentence...[37]

In discussing de Man's work, one must emphasize that for him close reading is, although endlessly productive, also in a sense, closed reading, in that it returns perpetually to the self-perpetuating domain of rhetoric for the terms in which it casts the problematic of consciousness and representation. Deconstruction is the demonstration of the dysfunctional linguistic conditions of cognition. This is perhaps to say that, however suggestive and apparently open the lines of conceptual enquiry in a reading by de Man, however inimitable and subtle its

readings of poetic, fictional and philosophical texts, it is hard
as a reader not to feel that there ultimately comes a point in his
essays where the *a priori* of the rhetorical problematic begins to
determine their argumentation and structure. At such a point
an assumed enquiring tone seems an earnest of a deeper manipulation, an assimilation of the reading of a text into a rhetorical dissection which vindicates his terminology. So, de Man's
work can often appear both familiar and incontrovertible in
its repeated stress on the undecidability of the distinction of
the rhetorical and the referential. If a Deleuzian close reading
would be in a different sense open, it would be in large part
because, to paraphrase a remark from *A Thousand Plateaus*, the
outside of language is internal to it. This section returns to this
point, but first, I offer a discussion of de Man's work in relation
to some points about its intellectual background. Particularly,
the aim is to draw out the different ontological thinking which
informs de Man's work, on the one hand, and Deleuze and
Guattari's, on the other, as well as to draw out different emphases in their linguistic thinking, taking their different uses of
J.L. Austin's *How to Do Things with Words* as a focus.

To take up this first point. In an essay on Paul de Man,
'*Setzung* and *Übersetzung*: Notes on Paul de Man', Rodolphe
Gasché traces the inwardness of de Man's poetics with the
Heideggerian destruction of the metaphysics of presence.[38] For
Heidegger, famously, what is present presupposes a presencing
or donation that must itself be concealed, even as it
dissimulates itself in what is present. Such a relation of constitution and deconstitution, and the complex temporality
involved, define an aporetic metaphysics which must refer the
present to that unpresent presenting by which the present is
given. De Man replays this, for Gasché, in a poetics which turns
on the impossibility of reading as a totalizing activity. Meaning
and its means are incompatible, and inseparable, in a similar
and irreducible way, since the form of understanding is given
by undecidable, exorbitant features of the rhetoric of language
that cannot themselves be understood, and certainly not in the
same act of understanding. The reader, and the writer as
reader, is caught between reading and the unreadable, within a
language that exceeds the forms of the human. Only in the

contemplation of rhetoric, within the interminable activity of reading, can thought wrest a problematic, even treacherous, sense of demystified autonomy out of its sense of finitude.

Secondly, Gasché's essay construes de Man's uses of the performative as being the crux of his work in ways which can be suggestively contrasted with Deleuze and Guattari's uses of the same term. For Gasché, de Man extends and complicates Austin's notion of the performative because of its amenability to description in terms of the kind of idealist metaphysics which de Man is combatting. So here, Gasché follows Benveniste's elucidation of the performative as a kind of positing: the performative can refer because it distinguishes within itself a function of self-reflexivity concerning itself as an act of language, from a dependent function of objective representation. Within representation, in short, construed in the performative, it must be possible to distinguish the means and the object of representation. And this is only possible if the means of representation, the act of enunciation, is essentially given to itself in a self-reflexive way. Reference depends on the distinguished self-reference of the subject who refers, one might say. The performative can refer to objects because it necessarily refers to itself, folding back on its own indicated and constitutive activity. Gasché sees de Man's uses of Austin's linguistic philosophy as a way of engaging with the field of subjectivity, then, as configured by the performative function of language. And what de Man does here, as most famously in *Allegories of Reading,* is to complicate the performative, so as to make undecidable or unreadable the distinctions between form and reference, subject and object, act and knowledge, aesthetics and thematics which it should constitute. The distinction between reflexivity and reference is in the process undone.

It is possible here briefly to indicate some of what appear to be the important differences between de Man and Deleuze and Guattari in these areas. The most obvious starting point is to emphasize the distinctive nature of Deleuze's ontology. Here I take my cue again from Michael Hardt, and his claim vis-à-vis the difference between Heidegger's pre-ontological or deontological thought, and Deleuze's reactivation of a different alternative to idealism:

> In effect, to contest the claims of an idealist ontology we do not
> need to go all the way to the opposite and propose a deontological
> perspective, but rather we can pursue the materialist ontological
> tradition as an alternative...[39]

and, to continue Hardt's commentary:

> There is nothing veiled about Deleuze's being; it is fully ex-
> pressed in the world...practice is what makes the constitution of
> being possible... The foundation of being, then, resides both on a
> corporeal and a mental plane, in the complex dynamics of
> behaviour; in the superficial interactions of bodies... The only
> nature available to ontological discourse is an absolutely artificial
> conception of nature, a hybrid nature, a nature produced in
> practice...[40]

In terms of Deleuze's own references to Heidegger, the lines
of Hardt's analyses are borne out. In *Difference and Repetition*,
Deleuze distinguishes what he sees as Nietzschean strains in
Heidegger, for instance in the construing of the ideality of
problems and questions in terms of their virtual reiterability,
their scope for differential repetition.[41] But this is to emphasize
a continuity with the materialist ontology that Hardt emphasizes, and against other features or interpretations of
Heidegger's work. Without getting drawn into the formidable
complexities of this, the main point here is that Deleuze draws
from philosophers like Spinoza, Bergson and Nietzsche a different ontological tradition, one that is not concerned with
idealist notions of ontological constitution, Kantian notions of
subjective transcendental determination, or Heideggerian notions of deontological foundation. The questions that emerge as
relevant here are basically two. What is the nature of such an
ontology, and what does it suggest for the description of reading?

The key to Deleuze's ontology, I have said in the last chapter,
is a notion of differentiation as defining the potential of Nature
and of things. Being is the productivity or expressivity of an
insistent and virtual power of self-difference. Like the theme
that subsists in variations, the virtual nature of a thing repeats
itself, in diverse actualizations. This nature is a heterogeneous
but inseparable 'set of relations' which repeats itself in its
various states, holding together its elements, and actualizing

different potentials.[42] This expressive movement of a thing is given in its duration, its qualitative alterations, the temporal multiplication of actual states. In terms of its states, a thing is composed as a multiplicity, also, in that it actualizes itself always differently each time, according to what it encounters. Yet in such chances are reiterated the necessity of its nature as a relatedness which is also always ultimately political, as well as speculative and ethical. The singular transformations which compose themselves from the thing's encounters actualize it as a deframed multiplicity of multiple lines of becoming. The multiplicities which are the thing as duration or state are, accordingly, unpredictable, surprising, blind, at once both forced and in principle autonomous, and opposed to pre-formed or superposed kinds of ordering (since they take form with what is outside). Hardt differentiates here between two kinds of multiplicity, which in a sense are the multiplicities of consciousness and representation on the one hand, a multi-plicity of predetermined order, and on the other, that which corresponds to Bergson's notion of living movement as self-differentiation, which Hardt refers to as 'the multiplicity of organization':

> The multiplicity of order is 'determinate' in that it is preformed and static; the multiplicity of organization is 'indeterminate' in that it is creative and original—organization is always unfore-seeable. Without the blueprint of order, the creative process of organization is always art...[43]

Chapter 4 of *A Thousand Plateaus* is concerned with distin-guishing these types of multiplicity in terms of language. Throughout the chapter, Deleuze and Guattari develop a pragmatics of language that involves notions of multiplicity, and which opposes a function of order in language to its capacity for unformed movements. The chapter ends with the following sentences:

> There are pass-words beneath order-words. Words that pass, words that are components of passage, whereas order-words mark stoppages or organized, stratified compositions. A single thing or word undoubtedly has this twofold nature: it is neces-sary to extract one from the other—to transform the compositions of order into components of passage...[44]

The ordering function of language displaces communication into a reduced and relative function. Language primarily is conceived as working to exact obedience, not to inform or communicate. Its main aim is the transmission of unspoken social imperatives. Its paradigm is the order-word: that, says Brian Massumi, which reduces language to the functions of that which 'goes without saying'.[45] Language working in such a way can only be understood, for Deleuze and Guattari, as exceeding its subjective moments, and as presupposing beyond them 'collective agents' who produce the forms of expression whereby the collective assemblage presupposed by language works on bodies to attribute to them 'incorporeal transformations'. A further example of this concept in *A Thousand Plateaus* is when a state of war is instantaneously introduced, incorporeally transforming the bodies concerned, and arranging them according to new attributes. Once again, the link between such statements and contexts is internal to language as an assemblage with two axes, an independent collective assemblage of enunciation which enunciates the expressed attributes of bodies, and a machinic assemblage of bodies which pertains to their physical symbioses and interminglings. To take up the example of the judge's pronouncement mentioned earlier: far from seeming to be most adequately described in terms of the performative and the subjectivity it appears to offer, such a pronouncement, for Deleuze and Guattari, would be one more case of an uncanny social ventriloquism, whereby a collective assemblage traverses individual bodies, and speaks through them.

In relation to de Man's account, the difference can be summarized briefly perhaps. De Man assimilates the illocutionary (what is done implicitly in and with language: asking, commanding, describing, and so on) to the performative (what is done by language as an expression of a subject: launching a ship, becoming married by speaking the marriage vows, and so on). The difference between the performative and illocutionary for de Man, then, does not seem a difference in kind, but a difference of degree, of explicitness, as Gasché claims it was for Austin himself, so that language crucially becomes dedicated to the possible activity of a subject. After all, as Gasché's analysis indicates, only if language aspires to be a function of the self-reflexive subject can rhetoric assume its full, confounding power. For Deleuze and Guattari, however, it appears in a contrary way that the fundamental function of the illocutionary is essential, if the analysis of language is to become a pragmatics, a politics. For the illocutionary is the function by which language carries out all sorts of implicit acts which are necessary for meaning, and which implicitly and perpetually refer to the operative requirements of context. These are the requirements which control me as speaker, and which refer implicitly to a collectivity that makes me work on their behalf. For Deleuze and Guattari, language is above all illocutionary, and the performative becomes merely a kind of special case of this characteristic. The necessarily social and pragmatic features of enunciation imply and convey the acts of a multiplicity which speaks through me, even when I say 'I' and perform an act in and by language. The performative, then, is not the paradigm of language as the domain of consciousness, but an effect of subjectivity within an impersonal assemblage which determines such subjective instances in language:

> what comes first is not an insertion of various individuated statements, or an interlocking of different subjects of enunciation, but a collective assemblage resulting in the determination of relative subjectification proceedings, or assignations of individuality and their shifting distributions within discourse. Indirect discourse is not explained by the distinction between subjects; rather, it is the assemblage, as it freely appears in this discourse, that explains all the voices present within a single voice…[46]

The Foucauldian elements in this discussion are unmistakeable.

Finally, to take up the point from the previous section as it arises again here: what distinctive notions of writing and reading arise from Deleuze and Guattari's discussions? Once again, the potential for political and aesthetic autonomy within such a state of affairs is inseparable from a deforming of the reciprocal instances of the form of content and the form of expression. In the process a creative variability can be freed on the plane of consistency which these forms presuppose, as in literary style and the operations of minor literature which draw on unformed materials of expression within the collective assemblage so as to construct lines of flight, passage, within the major language:

> The smallest interval is always diabolical; the master of meta-
> morphoses is opposed to the invariant hieratic king. It is as
> though an intense matter or a continuum of variation were freed,
> here in the internal tensors of language, there in the internal
> tensions of content. The idea of the smallest interval does not
> apply to figures of the same nature; it implies at least a curve and
> a straight line, a circle and a tangent. We witness a transfor-
> mation of substances and a dissolution of forms, a passage to the
> limit or flight from contours in favour of fluid forces, flows, air,
> light and matter, such that a body or a word does not end at a
> precise point. We witness the incorporeal power of that intense
> matter, the material power of that language...[47]

In his book, *Introducing Lyotard,* Bill Readings marshalled a deft
opposition between de Man's work and Lyotard's in ways that
are relevant here. For Readings, de Man's tendency was always
to reduce the political and futural aspect of the event by trans-
lating the temporal aporia of that which presents and that
which is presented into an epistemological impasse conveyed
through spatial metaphors. Such an emphasis blocks off a sense
of the critical power of the event as something happening
which cannot be understood. Without trying to minimize the
differences of vocabulary and drift here, there are important
points of similarity. In a similar way, the linguistic pragmatism
of Deleuze and Guattari maintains the status of linguistic acts as
political events which can counter the standardizing work of a
collective assemblage, to produce the shocks of the unrecognizable. Once again, the nature of such events is untimely, involving a critique and anticipating hitherto unconceived incorporeal transformations, new senses and expressions of bodies.

So then, the distinctively literary potential of a text for
Deleuze would seem to be inseparable from the reiterated expression of its unformed potential; that is, from the intervallic
manifestations of an undoing of those operative features of
form, subjectivity, and connectedness, syntax, plot which define a novel or poem in terms of the representative functions of
reading and genre. This is to emphasize or liberate the material
potential of words, their creative and infinite capacity to form
new relations, create new senses. A text is a body which is composed ultimately of elements which find their true expressiveness outside the formations which correspond to its official

generic features. In these ways, a text undoes reading as the property of a collected subject securing a communicative or interpretive relation to the text, and opens language repeatedly to its infinite nature to work upon us in surprising ways productive of new readings, and of unpredicted new assemblages of bodies, as in the onlooker, mother and child in Whitman's short poem.

Some Provisional Conclusions

These two preliminary chapters have sought to indicate something of how Deleuze's work, both alone and with Guattari, renews many themes in contemporary literary theory and criticism by providing a body of work which draws on many distinctively different kinds of ontological, epistemological, aesthetic, political and ethical resources, and which offers these in productive ways for the reading of literature.

3 |

Thomas Hardy—*Jude the Obscure*

'Frame and All'

This chapter is concerned with exploring how *Jude the Obscure* can be seen as an untimely text in the sense of Nietzsche's phrase, that is, one 'acting counter to our time and thereby acting on our time and, let us hope, for the benefit of a time to come...'[1] As this might suggest, this would be as a text which works to overturn from within the conventional forms of expression and content of nineteenth-century literary culture. Indeed, *Jude* is a novel which has always had the status of a kind of violent, destructive and unassimilable event, and its own bizarre, bleak and agonizing happenings, its effects of overdetermination, repetition, tragedy, and parody continue to provoke critical comment and to confound readers with undiminished intensity across a hundred years.[2] If *Jude* is a novel which strikingly has the status of a problem, it is because it divides our responses so utterly. In so many ways it seems to demand censure: for instance, in its laborious prosiness of style, or the oddly studied foursquare construction of paragraphs. As well there are all the ways in which the novel can seem boring, stagey, wooden, exasperating, and banal. It is by turns profoundly disappointing and diabolically comic in its portrayal of Jude's fate and relationships and the endless, mounting catalogue of distress involved. Yet at the same time, beyond these things, the narrative's events achieve effects of rawness that are simply overwhelming, as its language also retains the power to surprise us with a variety of fugitive, incidental emotional effects, of pathos, tenderness and physicality, for instance, that are absolute and heart-stopping. These paradoxes, accordingly, define the critic's task as one of accounting for the text's obscure ratio between the aesthetic outrages which the text perpetrates, and its power to discompose the reader and engage his or her diverse sympathies. In a large part this engagement works by the text's insistence on real potentials which are nonetheless denied expression in the world of the novel.

Linked to this, the discussion seeks to bring out how Hardy's text works to dissociate itself from the recognizable modes of nineteenth-century novelistic representation which it interrogates and displaces. More than this, however, the aim is to emphasize how the text converts the destructive aspects of its critique into powerful anticipations of literary modernity. Stuttering, repetitious as the novel is, it draws on unconscious powers of narrative intelligence, both critical and creative, which preserve an extraordinary power of implication. As an aspect of this, this chapter looks at how the novel time and again stages the undoing of Jude's mystified hopes of connection, within the disjoined and intensive spaces of particular scenes. The aesthetic disarticulations of the text force complex kinds of response which generate simultaneous and divergent lines of reading. Further, these features of the text ultimately come to bear with a kind of productive critical scrutiny on the text's own workings, so that an important aspect of the novel is the way in which the text offers an allegory of its own resistance to readerly comprehension. This is connected to the way in which the writing also seems to exceed and outrun authorial consciousness, and to define something of the enigmatic status of the novel for Hardy himself.

Where this discussion departs from a more familiar kind of deconstructive reading, however, is that this situation is not seen solely as an epistemological impasse, but as the means by which the text can work as minor literature, anticipating as yet unactualized communities and times. The novel in these ways intensifies our sense of *Jude*'s status as a text of a time between times, one which involves a repetition of a past whose possibilities of meaning and affection are now perceived as terminated or decayed, and a repetition of a future whose intensive features must unfold out of the singularity of this interval into the different and the unknown, into the new, unforeseen linkages and expressions which are recurrently signalled in the text. It can be said that the novel raises disappointment to a new power, so that irony, and black humour even, become the means not only for a subverting of conventional novelistic representations and resolutions, but also the means for the novel's repetition of hope itself as an ineradicable structure of response and experience. Hope is *the* main emotion, after all, which the text engenders, even as it is unactualizable within the novel's world.

As a preliminary way into these aspects of the text, consider the seemingly improvised scene towards the end of the first part of *Jude the Obscure*, which Hardy's narrator interpolates into the narrative. Here Jude finds in the broker's shop the photograph of himself which he had given to Arabella. The picture had been a wedding present, inscribed to Arabella, and Jude buys it, takes it home, and burns it. The episode is in every sense possessed by redundancy and superfluity. It merely reiterates an estrangement that demands no recapitulation, and the scene lacks any linkage to anything that comes before or after—we have never heard of the picture before, and will not again. Instead, the episode seems obviously motivated to represent once again, through the destruction of the picture, the superseding of the self-representation which the picture represents, the lapsing of the verbal promises which were Jude and Arabella's wedding vows, and of the face to face which the gift of such a photograph is dedicated to maintain. The episode merely offers confirmation of Jude's own unnecessary status, but as such it appears itself as a peculiarly wasteful and disjoined addition to the text. It emphasizes once again the interruption of the lifetime project which his marriage was, and in itself leads nowhere beyond Jude's wasting of more time and money. So, it might be said, an unnecessary scene which bears on an experience which unnecessarily indicates Jude's own unnecessary status.

While such repetitious and disjoined scenes in the novel in important ways dissolve its representative adequacy, they nonetheless also retain all the more the powerful and paradoxical force of the untimely. Hence the ratio in the passage and its language between a certain exhaustive laboriousness, and a strange, intense attentiveness and pathos which seems at work behind the words, and which catches the leading edge of the reader's attention:

> The utter death of every tender sentiment in his wife, as brought home to him by this mute and undesigned evidence of her sale of his portrait and gift, was the conclusive little stroke required to demolish all sentiment in him. He paid the shilling, took the photograph away with him, and burnt it, frame and all, when he reached his lodging.[3]

The passage is marked by repetition, and by an alternation of modes. The first sentence is wholly unnecessary, all frame, all tedious expository syntax and bloated tautology ('utter death', 'tender sentiment', 'mute and undesigned evidence', 'portrait and gift', 'conclusive…to demolish…'). The second sentence is all reductive externalized description, which eclipses the pseudo-analysis of the first sentence by implying all that that sentence spells out of Jude's disappointment ('He paid the shilling, took the photograph away with him, and burnt it, frame and all, when he reached his lodging'). The language in this way itself comes to stage the superseding of a novelistic means of representation amenable to social recognition and narrative continuity. Through juxtaposition and an excess of elaboration the language of identification, interpretation and evaluation is undone, disjoined, discarded, 'frame and all', its syntheses destroyed as the narrative is given over to new beginnings. So at the end of this chapter, Jude rediscovers the milestone. Its inscription refers him again to Christminster, and 'lit in his soul a spark of the old fire…'[4]

So, accordingly, the discussion that follows tries to account for the text's effectiveness, and explores its various means of being given over to an increasingly energetic, and apparently perverse, destruction of the retrospective logic, the reactive framings and forces, of Victorian fiction. As a preliminary statement of what is involved here, it is as if an experienced fate of repetition, of ironic disjunction, or, at an affective or a dramatic level, of disappointment or alienation, coexists with, draws Hardy's text into, a kind of wilfully destructive repetition. This would be a form of *amor fati*, which seeks to overcome the laws of this fate through an intensified involvement within it. The discussion which follows develops its reading in part in relation to Deleuze's account of Nietzsche's eternal return, as involving, ethically, a willed repetition of repetition, and as offering a way of understanding the issues here. For Deleuze's Nietzsche, through a compounding of fate the will participates paradoxically by way of destructiveness in an untimely creativity which anticipates through feeling in the advent of an unknown and illegible time to come. The will is 'transformed into a power of affirmation' and diversity through a willed negation, an energetic destruction.[5]

In terms of the novel's drama one could take as an example of this 'active destruction'[6] not merely its many floutings of aesthetic good form, its discarding of the grammars and codes of the past, but also its engagement with tragedy and self-destruction, as in Jude's last rainy suicidal visit to Sue, consumed by the sense that 'the time was not ripe for us!'[7] Like the man who wants to perish in the prologue to *Thus Spoke Zarathustra*, for Jude ultimately having nowhere to go enables him to exist as a 'bridge and not a goal'.[8] As this whole discussion might suggest, Jude's obscurity is most fully to be accounted for in terms of the unrecognizable forms of life which his experience anticipates, the times yet to come to which the text recurrently signals.

To describe the text's combinings of destruction and anticipation in terms of Nietzsche's notion of the eternal return allows one to identify ideas of obscurity or modernity as the inmost resources of the spirit which participates in a deframing, an ontological movement that cannot be represented or understood. It unfolds within an interval that exceeds the hegemony of reading, of conceptual thought, and recognition. And it is this breaching of the generically limiting work of territory, conservation and memory in the novel which defines the minoritarian-becoming of the novel. This is effected by the novel's deformations of form and expression, its drawing of the reader out of him or herself into relation with Jude.

These comments define the links between Hardy and Proust, Woolf, and Lawrence, each of whom acknowledged Hardy as a great precursor. They allow, also, for a certain access into Deleuze and Guattari's identification of Hardy as one among many Anglo-American novelists who refuse to use literary art as a refuge, as a means of recoiling into rehearsals of 'subjectivity, of consciousness and memory, of the couple and conjugality'. Against this, for writers from Hardy to Lawrence, Melville to Miller,

> art is never an end in itself; it is only a tool for blazing life lines, in other words all those real becomings that are not produced only in art, and all of those active escapes that do not consist in fleeing into art, taking refuge in art, and all those positive deterritorializations that never reterritorialize on art, but instead sweep it away with them toward the realm of the asignifying, asubjective, and faceless...[9]

Obscurity

The ideas of obscurity and modernity both involve dislocation in terms that go along with the discussion above. A condition of obscurity—peering into the dark, attempting to understand a sign, feeling on the margins of a social group—holds a person in an interval, a moment of painful suspense in which implicitly the articulations, identifications and clarities of the past have nothing to offer. Instead, there is simply the divided experience of a present whose meaning is unclear, and of a future which is formless and uncertain. And such a description could obviously be applied directly to the idea of modernity, as employed in this novel, where experience dwindles to a past that must be forgotten (since its modes are superseded), a future that cannot be predicted, and the confused intensities and movements of the interim.

Jude the Obscure is, in obvious ways, a text whose drama is a remorseless reiteration and intensification of such states of dissociation. Jude presses on, necessarily forgetting his past errors as he aims to find a home and function within the world of the novel. However, in the ironic travelogue of the text, his progress is continually interrupted, and he is returned to the unhappy stations and new departures of what increasingly emerges as a fate of non-belonging enjoined upon him by the novel's world. This fate of disconnection, of a deterritorialized existence in a time between times, does not merely manifest itself in the kind of parodic anti-narrative which it makes of Jude's hopes, however, but also in the ways the text comes to be increasingly a kind of troubled meditation on this state of things. A reflexive and disheartened musing comes to further inhibit the onward press of narrative, the narrative recoiling, as in the example above of the picture, into an introverted exploration of its own formal perplexities.

Jude in this way can be seen as what can be termed a text of the outside, and of a time to come. Its events are bordered from without and divided from within by the 'margin of the unexpressed' in Woolf's phrase about Hardy (taken up by Roger Ebbatson as the title of his book on Hardy).[10] This is a phrase which I construe here, for my own purposes, as in a large part referring to the '*still* unexpressed' and so to the text's production, on the far side of irony as it were, of a sense of virtual potentials of self-expression and change that are real, though as yet unactualized. The leverage which the text exerts through repetition against the customary modes and syntheses of the nineteenth-century novel becomes the condition of the text's insistence on the singularity of Jude's problematic experience and status. Jude, indefinite and open as a character in his deterritorialized status, is endlessly susceptible to intimations of relatedness. For Jude himself, these intimations, in the details of his encounters, always bear on ideal hopes of association. However, he is unable to translate these into a lived experience because the social order of the world resists his attempts to rise above his obscure situation, and the contingencies of his displaced and penurious existence. Jude responds to what seem the signals of productive association, a means of finding oneself, but the momentary transports, the suggestions of becoming-different, that are produced here are shown to involve a fatal absent-mindedness, subject to the ironies and reductions of circumstances:

> Suddenly there came along this wind something towards him—a message from the place, from some soul residing there, it seemed. Surely it was the sound of bells, the voice of the city, faint and musical, calling to him, 'We are happy here!'
>
> He had become entirely lost to his bodily situation during this mental leap, and only got back to it by a rough recalling...[11]

Within the world of this novel, such effects of music and community merely encourage a fated and forlorn hope of relatedness, as, again, to take another musical example, when Jude visits the composer of the hymn that had moved him so much, Jude intends to confide in him only to discover that the man is moving into the more lucrative intoxications of the wine trade:

> It took Jude more than by surprise that the man with the soul was thus and thus; and he felt he could not open up his confidences...[12]

And, similarly, when Jude's soul can be said finally to leave his body, in this text it is to the ironic sounds of music, the bells and organ concert and waltz which punctuate his dying remarks. The wrenching black humour in these episodes, however, has as its background a belief in the inevitability of the projections to which music appears to testify. The more Hardy piles on the satire, the more the ghastly hollowness of the laughter has as its condition the pathos and intensity of an affective susceptibility now increasingly dissociated from any belief in its realization, yet which must repeat itself. As a result of this, the remorseless intensification of disappointment has the effect of testifying to its opposite, to an intensified sense that life is impossible without hope, as dissonance evokes a counter-image of harmony perhaps. Further, of course, things end badly in this text, its movements are constantly interrupted and fruitless, but the reader's sense of the novel's tragic elements is inseparable from a sense of its being a text that in all sorts of ways anticipates other times, other communities and ways of relating. This is so even as these remain essentially provisional and fated anticipations, uncompleted ambitions, virtualities that subsist in the irresolvable complications or obscurities of the text, its thwarted reachings out and forward. These features ensure that *Jude the Obscure* remains always a text in movement, a text of becoming. A text, finally, that is dedicated to maintaining an open and unfolding interval beyond the major forms of fiction which its modes of irony and parody work to discard.

These aspects of the novel are evident from its opening:

> The schoolmaster was leaving the village, and everybody seemed sorry. The miller at Cresscombe lent him the small white tilted cart and horse to carry his goods to the city of his

Lines of Flight

destination, about twenty miles off, such a vehicle proving of quite sufficient size for the departing teacher's effects. For the schoolhouse had been partly furnished by the managers, and the only cumbersome article possessed by the master, in addition to the packing case of books, was a cottage-piano that he had bought at an auction during the year in which he thought of learning instrumental music. But the enthusiasm having waned he had never acquired any skill in playing, and the purchased article had been a perpetual trouble to him ever since in moving house.

The rector had gone away for the day, being a man who disliked the sight of changes. He did not mean to return till the evening, when the new school-teacher would have arrived and settled in, and everything would be smooth again.

The blacksmith, the farm bailiff, and the schoolmaster himself were standing in perplexed attitudes in the parlour before the instrument. The master had remarked that even if he got it into the cart he should not know what to do with it on his arrival at Christminster, the city he was bound for, since he was only going into temporary lodgings just at first.

A little boy of eleven, who had been thoughtfully assisting in the packing, joined the group of men, and as they rubbed their chins he spoke up, blushing at the sound of his own voice: 'Aunt have got a great fuel-house, and it could be put there, perhaps, till you've found a place to settle in, sir.'[13]

The novel begins with a static scene, yet anticipates transition and movement. Phillotson, along with almost everyone else in the scene, is identified, through the use of the definite article, within the context of the village he is nonetheless leaving ('The schoolmaster was leaving the village... The miller... The rector... The blacksmith, the farm bailiff...'). The articles abound indeed, as the most obvious markers of a kind of excessive framing which affects the prose in other ways too, as, for instance, in the laboured use of postmodifying phrases and clauses of every kind. It would be easy to multiply examples of the narrator's pursuit of explication and definition here, a pursuit by which the prose is given an air at once leaden and anxious. Through being overdrawn, the text's terms of familiar representation appear hollowed out, at once both confirmed and undermined. Such prosiness on the face of it, then, exacerbates a narrative insecurity through the very attempts to compensate for it.

The complexities in this account are further suggestive in relation to the medley of emotional effects conveyed by the prose. There is humour and pathos most obviously, but also a less easily describable and lowering sense, very characteristic of *Jude*, of a narrator caught within a means or scheme of representation which appears both necessary and unworkable, both time-honoured and provisional. For the reader this settles out as the sense of a narrator caught between an inescapable heavy-handedness, and a kind of mounting inner frustration at this, a frustration which constitutes a kind of reaction, a kind of demoralized counter-current in the emotional swirl of the text. Exasperation and hopelessness are perhaps the most readily describable emotions here, and as this account suggests, they work in ways which are at once pervasive, involuntary, unacknowledged and unpredicted. As with Phillotson and his piano, the 'cumbersome article', which he is powerless to play or to transport or to locate in his 'temporary lodgings', the narrative seems in an important sense perplexed by a novelistic means of expression for which the narrator no longer has conviction or enthusiasm, and which appears ill adapted to the requirements of altering circumstances. And so when Jude is first picked out in this context, through the indefinite article ('A little boy of eleven'), the narrative not only anticipates Jude's ultimate lack of social identification, but focuses questions of language on the unnamed boy, who even dramatizes them ('...he spoke up, blushing at the sound of own voice...').

In these ways, discontinuities and indeterminacies at the level of language appear as verbal correlates of Jude's obscure fate. And so also, to take this further, as Jude comes to an increasingly bitter knowledge that he cannot overcome the ironic circuits in which he is trapped, so the narrative involves all kinds of bitter effects—of parody, laying it on thick, and the *mise en abîme*, in which the displacements of form become not merely a critical matter, but implicitly a matter of criticism within the text itself. A kind of perplexed reflexive crease emerges once again here, as with the destroyed frame mentioned at the beginning, as scenes and language stage troubled and suspended intervals of reading for narrator and reader, as for character.

Modernity

Nietzsche famously identified the true modernity intrinsic to life with the need to forget, the 'faculty of oblivion' which creates the limited functional power of mental activity, at once positively repressing the traces of the past, and preserving the readiness of consciousness to react in the openness of the present.[14] The power of forgetting is to erase anteriority, the past, and to liberate the creative powers of mind by overcoming memory, history, retrospection. Wrote Nietzsche in his *Untimely Meditations*:

> ... Forgetting is essential to action of any kind...it is possible to live almost without memory...but it is altogether impossible to live at all without forgetting...[15]

> ... As he who acts is...always without a conscience, so he is also without knowledge; he forgets most things so as to do one thing, he is unjust towards what lies behind him, and he recognizes the rights only of that which is now to come into being...[16]

Blindness to what has been is the screening condition of the action of the mind. It operates at a leading edge of excited awareness, eluding personality, and scarcely deserves the name of consciousness that Nietzsche gives it in *The Genealogy of Morals*.[17] The pertinence of this to *Jude the Obscure* is clear. The Victorian novel as a form can be seen, for all its real and constituent divisions, as ostensibly dedicated to the processes of memory and reflection, to a retroactive completion of the dramatic complications it played out. In many of its overt and fundamental workings it sought to bring the present and future within the extended orbit of the past, as Dickens's novels overcome alienation by reuniting the child with parents, real or surrogate. The future as a genuine dimension is there reduced to a regressive synthesis with what has been, the indeterminacies and disarticulations of becoming are overcome by the sustaining return of what one has known, of extant social codes. Hardy's text, against this, presents memory as intolerable for Jude, emphasizing throughout the character's need, as it were, to remember to forget. The character must keep moving away, within the nomadic interval of the present, beyond the superseded frames or discarded grammars of the past and the dashed hopes to which they testify.

Further, Deleuze's reading of Nietzsche, as shall be shown, emphasizes the creative potential of such destructive movements, in their opening up of new potentialities of experience and writing. An initial blind movement within the obscure, dislocated interval of modernity leads to a transmutation of the negative—the creation of new values, and the overcoming of memory as the controlling principle of individual action and identity. *Jude,* as has been suggested, is a text marked by a deepening reflexive sense of a potential fate of radical obscurity. It comes increasingly to participate in this, through a variety of devices of overdetermination and self-interrogation which open language to indetermination. In this last respect, Hardy's text becomes an engagement through repetition of writing with its own limits. Through the repetition of a problem writing takes the form of a question. More specifically, it is Deleuze's reading of Nietzsche's notion of the eternal return that is central here. Deleuze discovers in the eternal return an ethical principle which offers ontology its ultimate resource, since it is in the ethical selection of the eternal return that is discovered the power of affirmation that is inherent to becoming.[18] Accordingly, in the eternal return the denegation of the forces of becoming that is operative in the nihilistic work of socially reactive, anamnestic forces comes to grief itself. The negations which are intrinsic to the conservative work of memory are themselves negated in a destruction whose import is ultimately creative:

> Only the eternal return can complete nihilism *because it makes negation a negation of reactive forces themselves*... In self-destruction reactive forces are themselves denied and led to nothingness. This is why self-destruction is said to be an active operation, an '*active destruction*'... Active negation or active destruction is the state of strong spirits which destroy the reactive in themselves, submitting it to the test of the eternal return and submitting themselves to this test even if it entails willing their own decline...[19]

> It is...by repetition that forgetting becomes a positive power and the unconscious a positive, superior, unconscious...forgetting as

> a force is an integral part of the lived experience of eternal
> return...[20]

> And what would the eternal return be, if we forgot that it is a
> vertiginous movement endowed with a force: not one which
> causes the return of the Same in general, but one which selects,
> one which expels as well as creates, destroys as well as pro-
> duces? Nietzsche's leading idea is to found the repetition in the
> eternal return at once on the death of God and the dissolution of
> the self...[21]

Throughout the novel, the importance of forgetting as the
repeated disruption of that in memory which would bind and
diminish the force of the present is everywhere evident. However necessary such a forgetting is, though, it is always itself
everywhere thwarted in this text, as are all explicit rehearsals
of the future, by being folded back ironically into that pattern
of the past which it had sought to escape. Ambition, kicking
over the traces, is fated always to return to this parodically
reflexive, intermittent sense of the inescapability of the past
whose failures it repeats. Everywhere in the novel Jude attempts again and again to overcome disappointment by a new
scheme, forgetting his past errors and seeking a new beginning.
But his attempts to compensate for the foreign nature of circumstances leads to disillusion and a sense of painful exclusion:
Jude feeds the birds and is punished and sacked by the farmer;
Phillotson leaves him; Vilbert swindles him; Arabella deceives
him; Sue frustrates him; he walks out onto the ice but it won't
crack beneath his feet; Christminster snubs him; his working
colleagues make him feel he must resign from the Artisans'
Mutual Improvement Society, and so on. Such a pattern in the
text is too familiar to need labouring here, as are all the other
features of the novel with which it combines—the decline of
narrative continuities into a paratactic, repetitive series of dead
ends; the ironic travelogue of the plot; the arrangements of
characters, scenes and incidents and detail to interrupt and
disappoint Jude's hopes. Jude's tale is one of social and personal dissociation, in which Hardy undoes the hegemony of
memory as a control of Victorian novelistic representation.
Here memory is consigned by the very force of repetition to
a reduced, ironic function, one that undoes, increasingly des-

perately, the very continuities of narrative and selfhood which it had generically underpinned. Memory is merely a register of failed association, and a function of interruption, and so works against its function as a paradigmatic synthetic principle working towards the representation of a recognizable and communicable image of society and self.

This temporal problematic has obvious and illuminating points of contact with Lyotard's identification of the postmodern as the inmost potential of a truly modern art. For Lyotard, also, modern art is predicated on exile, forgetting or dissociation, which are the conditions of a hopeful subjective freedom, of a dedication to new syntheses. The complexity of this description is importantly increased by the ways in which, for Lyotard, the postmodern coexists with the modern, being at once inseparable from it, incompatible with it, and necessary to it. The postmodern activity of reflective judgment maintains the provisionality of the projects framed by modernity by subjecting them to a critical vigilance. It articulates through a significant affect the disjunctions between the ideal and the real which are covered or repressed in the necessary illusions of modernity. In this way the postmodern ensures the recurrence of the essential newness of the modern, its truly 'nascent state[s]'.[22] There is then a ratio here which is suggestive for the study of *Jude the Obscure*, between a modern attitude given over to narrative unity, yet based on a prior interruption, first, and, second, the internal interruption of this by a further attitude, the postmodern. Although belated, the postmodern returns the modern to what was always its most intrinsic temporality, and emphasizes what is illusory in the accord which the mind mourned, or sought to introduce, between how things are and how they could or should be. Without complicating this further, there are some remarks by Lyotard on this whose terms helpfully anticipate aspects of the following discussion of *Jude the Obscure*:

> The postmodern would be that which in the modern invokes the unpresentable in presentation itself, which refuses the consolation of correct forms, refuses the consensus of taste permitting a common experience of nostalgia for the impossible, and inquires into new presentations—not to take pleasure in them but to better produce the feeling that there is something unpresentable...[23]

More directly to relate this scheme to the novel itself, and to its drama initially—if Jude lives a modern attitude in his partly nostalgic dedication to an adventure of meaning, he encounters an unlivable postmodernity in the advent of a disruptive sense of the impossibility of this. As far as the temporal scheme of narrative is concerned, the postmodern would emerge as a kind of interpolation, narratively or psychologically, which arises from within the connective work of the modern attitude to confound it intermittently with a painful sense of ironic disjunction. The postmodern is a sense which reflects on what has been necessarily repressed in the pressings on of modernity, even as the postmodern sets up the possibility of their renewal, and transformation. So for Jude, the yielding of his hopes to cruel experience accentuates not only the resumption of his search for a defining context, but also, prior to this, a critical and conflicting sense of the loss of unity in the self. The provisional premises of a new life are revisited anachronistically by what they sought to exclude, or thought they had left behind, as when Arabella, for instance, in a familiar pattern in the text, turns up again at Jude's lodgings; or when Jude unwittingly revisits with Sue the hotel he had visited with Arabella; or when Little Father Time arrives in Jude's life. Such interruptive revisitings of the present by the past define a critical moment which carries with it a certain bitter knowledge, then, of the illusions that had inhabited the initial interruption by which character or narrator had dedicated themselves to new beginnings. Memory returns to criticize forgetting, and to confront it with what it had sought to repress.

As a further and relatively straightforward example of these things, remember the young Jude, in the first chapter, on the novel's first foggy morning. The orphan Jude recoils, with 'the quiver in his lip now', from the loneliness of Phillotson's departure to peer down the ancient well at the 'shining disk of quivering water'. Jude's gesture is a compulsive and introverted one which only momentarily and ambivalently appeases his sense of 'the pricks of life'.[24] Inevitably, Jude's search for distraction is disappointed, as his reverie is broken in on by his aunt who further chastises him. The overcoming of memory again is defined as commensurate with a relapse into illusion. Jude in the blankness of his loneliness cannot help but look for some sort of compensating reflection in the novel's world, but he comes as always to the sense that it returns no echo or reflection to thought or whimsy—that its shinings offer a merely illusory transcendence, that its quiverings are not those of any sympathetic accord. The potential consolations and illuminations of Jude's action appear ultimately to redouble this interpolated and critical sense, one that deepens throughout the novel, of the unfitness of consciousness and world. The solitary boy is returned by his actions and his aunt's interruption to an enhanced negative knowledge of the 'obliterations' to which the ambitions and records of human history and identity are subject, as in the 'obliterated graves...commemorated by eighteen-penny cast-iron crosses warranted to last five years...' with which the first chapter ends.[25] This is an image of human dissociation that encompasses all human meanings and narratives, and that confronts the memory which is the vehicle of the insight with an image of its own erasure. For Jude the chapter ends by suggesting once again his need to forget the bleak knowledge he has recognized, even as the second chapter ends with the immemorial 'bleak open down',[26] associated with a lost and anonymous historical multitude, that separates Jude from the far off city of Christminster.

So then, *Jude the Obscure* is a novel which explores ultimately the interspace of modernity as a critical one in various senses. Past forms can be perceived as such, even as they become all the more necessary and inescapable. Disjunction or displacement, as an aspect of its modernity, possesses this text in every aspect. In *Jude the Obscure*, repetition does not conserve but destroys, and anticipates an as yet unrealized future. The text in many aspects produces effects of mobility—between the superseded and the intensities of the yet unknown—like those that Deleuze notes in Kierkegaard and Nietzsche, where philosophical works aspire to deformations which shock sensibility and animate thought:

> ... It is not enough...for them to propose a new representation of movement... Rather, it is a question of producing within the work a motion capable of affecting the mind outside of all representation...[27]

In terms of the text's own famous power to move, a power that seems at odds with its representative inadequacies, I have stressed here how memory as a conventional novelistic function becomes ironically inverted in ways that anticipate its own demise. As a merely reflexive means, by way of which failures of representation are represented and repeated in a deepening spiral of thwarted will and interiority, memory merely functions to reproduce and intensify the emotional atmosphere of baffled and increasingly desperate alienation which pervades the text. John Bayley suggests this in his comment on how this novel and *The Well-Beloved* possess an 'air of no further place to go'.[28] For Jude there can be no fulfilling representation in the world of the novel, merely a deepening predicament of introversion.

'More in a Book than the Author Consciously Puts There'

This section is concerned with exploring in more detail the problematic of reading in the text, beginning in this section with the very literal senses in which many of Hardy's readers have found the text unreadable, and moving on to Hardy's own intriguing authorial anxiety and puzzlement before his final novel.

There are many reasons why the novel's readers have felt the novel to be unreadable. The hypotactic logic of good form and realistic representation is overcome by the derealizing stutterings, parodic spirals, and fragmenting intensities of the plot. The increasing use of explicitly repetitive devices is perhaps the most overt manifestation of this aspect of the text— Jude returns to Christminster, remarries Arabella, comes across Tinker Tailor again and again, and so on. Suspense as the normalizing time of narrative is itself suspended by the jamming to which these repetitions subject the narrative.

This is perhaps most notoriously evident in the presentation of the deaths of the children and of Jude himself. It is the combination in the reader's response at such moments that defines a true unreadability. The reader is divided between something that is in its presentation at the same time unbelievable, provoking outrage or disgust, and unreadable in the further and incompatible sense of producing unassimilable intensities and shocks. In such moments, the reader is caught between the factitiousness of narrative pattern and the unmanageable, violent emotions that the text's events produce. To take the former example. On the one hand, here the artifice is wholly clear—the children have been dreamed up pages before, apparently to die merely for plot purposes; that is, to dissociate Jude and Sue by the unmanageable force of this new crisis. In this response we seem to stand outside the novel, to see its construction of events, its production of effects, its frame of representation. Once again, the pattern stands out with a crudity that seems incompatible with narrative realism. Yet at the same time, when responding to the detail and language of the episode the reader feels an emotional power that is overwhelming. In this aspect the deaths seem beyond belief because they have the wholly stunning impact of tragedies that owe nothing to books. Hardy's early readers responded to this accurately enough as a breach of novelistic decorum: such tragedies may take place in life, but we do not want them in books. But the simple point is the dislocation involved in our responses—the deaths are unbelievable: incredible in the first sense, unbearable in the other.

In this respect it is striking to note how the issue of unreadability is raised by and in Hardy's own repeated authorial ruminations on *Jude* in the preface, the postscript and the letters. In his preface to the first edition of *Jude the Obscure*, he refers to the 'difficulty of coming to an early decision in the matter of a title', and to the two provisional titles which were 'successively adopted' before the eventual choice, 'deemed on the whole the best', as well as 'one of the earliest thought of'.[29] As with so many of Hardy's remarks about the novel, what is circumspect in the tone of his comments appears assumed, inseparable from a bemusement which eventually works its way out at the level of statement. His use of the master's voice lacks conviction and intellectual mobility, evident in a falling away of reason as the remarks subside into a greater tentativeness about his control of his text. This can be seen in the closing remarks of the postscript to Jude, that 'no doubt there can be

more in a book than the author consciously puts there',[30] or in
his famous letter to Gosse:

> Your review is the most discriminating that has yet appeared. It
> required an artist to see that the plot is almost geometrically con-
> structed—I ought not to say constructed, for, beyond a certain
> point, the characters necessitated it, & I simply let it come.[31]

The praising of Gosse's acumen is self-bolstering, but once again
it is a deeper uncertainty which comes to overtake the passage.
This is even more obvious in an equally famous letter to Gosse:

> Of course the book is all contrasts—or was meant to be in its
> original conception. Alas, what a miserable accomplishment it
> is, when I compare it with what I meant to make it!—e.g. Sue
> and her heathen gods set against Jude's reading the Greek testa-
> ment; Christminster academical, Christminster in the slums;
> Jude the saint, Jude the sinner; Sue the pagan, Sue the saint;
> marriage, no marriage; etc, etc.[32]

John Bayley writes of an impression of 'disingenuousness'[33] in
Hardy's comments in the above and other similar passages.
Certainly, it is true that there is a protective self-consciousness
and pathos in the various elements of these oscillations which
can compromise a direct response to what Hardy says. However, this self-protectiveness does not seem to motivate the
statements so much as to derive from them, as part of a reflexive recognition of a genuine and discomfiting difficulty which
cannot ultimately be mastered or disguised. The eager intention to comprehend the workings of the text subsides into an
ironic and deeply undermining recognition of intractability, a
knowledge whose revelation is the source of the edge of intellectual panic in the remarks, and of each repeated attempt to
overcome or cover or avoid it. Nothing could be harder to describe than this, because the self-reflexive mode in these texts
precisely defines the loss of unity in the authorial self, and of
self-consciousness, while mocking or haunting each of the attempted unities or identities of the narrative with intimations
of their negative image.

'They Were Entirely in Darkness'

This chapter has so far explored some of the ways in which the
writing in *Jude the Obscure* becomes adequate to an intensive

time of becoming, through the repetition of kinds of dissociation from the past. Language itself becomes opened in this
process to its potential as a domain of virtual sense beyond pre-
arranged or logically recuperable possibilities of meaning. Interpretation here can only be bemused by what within this text
repeatedly interrupts the order of narrative and style, and ex-
ploits effects of obscurity as language's inmost potential. Reading is challenged to move beyond the assumptions of received
meaning, in all the phenomenological, semiotic and sociological
senses of that phrase, to be adequate to the voyage in indeterminacy which is the crucial mode of the text. In this way it can
be said to open the untimely interval in which future modes
of writing and reading are anticipated, or, putting it another
way, in which their oldest potentials are repeated.

As an aspect of this, throughout *Jude the Obscure*, Hardy's narrative language is haunted by a lack of resolution. Words seem
uncertain in their contexts, provisional, ambivalent, opaque or
rudimentary, often cut across and truncated by more immediate currents of involvement or curtailed by perfunctoriness or
laboriousness. In one way these effects of style can be seen as
an outcome of a striving for interpretive narrative mastery in
Jude, and reveal the lack of the desired dexterity, lucidity, or
capacity for synthesis. Hardy's often disparaged tendency to a
certain prolix exhaustiveness and a narrative marking of time
becomes critical in this text, by virtue of their indication of the
defeat of a narrative ambition which would overcome disjunction.

Such features of the narrative, as has been suggested, can be
detected in the smallest detail of language and scene, as in the
following brief example, where Jude meets Sue for the first
time after the preliminaries of the photograph with which Jude
is infatuated, the series of rather voyeuristic glimpses and anec-
dotes, and the flurry of letters and notes. Although this is in a
dramatic way a first meeting, it has been presaged by all kinds
of earlier representation:

> The broad street was silent, and almost deserted, although it was
> not late. He saw a figure on the other side, which turned out to be
> hers, and they both converged towards the cross-mark at the
> same moment.[34]

Concerned with a meeting, this is an episode that is equally haunted by the possibility of divergences of all kinds. It is a matter not merely of what is fateful in the meeting of Jude and Sue at the martyr's memorial, but also of what eludes the obvious determination of the writing. The affective undertow of the passage in part derives again from a backwash of possibilities of meaning which are posited by the syntax, but which it cannot recover, and which, although strictly impossible, knit and reknit at the margin of the reader's consciousness, issuing there without surviving. Once again it is an overdetermination that liberates the fluid potentials of meaning that it seems designed to contain. How much clearer, for instance, were clarity an appropriate aim here, the second sentence would be if the italicized words had been left out:

> He saw a figure on the other side, *which turned out to be hers,* and
> they *both* converged towards the cross-mark *at the same moment...*

As it is, although the reader makes sense of such a sentence, it is at the cost of effectively deleting such words, and the divergent possibilities of meaning which they throw up. Otherwise, such,meanings could delay the reader indefinitely within an interval of reading. There the reader would meditate, for instance, on the idea that there could be a distinction, and hence a convergence, between Sue and the disembodied and unattributed *'figure...which turned out to be hers'*; or that there could be a convergence which is only *ever* a *progress* 'towards'; or that there could be a convergence which is not that of *both* figures, or that takes place at *different* moments. As it is, the coming together of Jude and Sue is delayed, and they walk along in parallel lines (as did Arabella and Jude in the passage which described their first meeting, as they walked along the two sides of the river):

> They walked on in parallel lines, and waiting her pleasure, Jude
> watched till she showed signs of closing in, when he did
> likewise, the place being where the carriers' carts stood in the
> daytime...[35]

More incidentally, as so often in the text a delicacy of feeling is momentarily suggested here in the phrase 'waiting her pleasure', whose effect is agonizingly touching within the larger sense of suspense and foreboding which possesses the text. And so, in an obvious sense, the scene at the martyr's memorial is a postponement of the coming together of Jude and Sue, until they arrive at 'the place where the carriers' carts stood in the daytime'. The scene itself becomes, accordingly, defined as an interval where a relation is yet to be begun, and yet which seems also a repetition.

This example is important here, further, because it is typical of many such scenes in the novel where Hardy's narrator will append, or seem to extemporize, an episode which leads no-where and which appears at odds with any narrative conti-nuity, however speculative or provisional. Nonetheless, these inconsequential scenes often condense, as we have seen, within their own mysterious compass a kind of critical commentary on the text's ostensible narrative ambitions. So then, from with-in the narrative there emerges a critical dimension which off-sets the projects of narrative, experience and language in their obvious functions, interpolating obscure intermissions whose disjunctive potentials could prolong us indefinitely were we not bound to repress their confusions in a renewed commit-ment to reading on.

The final passage here comes at the end of Chapter 1 of Part IV. Jude has just left Sue, parting under the window sill. But on this last page he returns for some unknown motive, and sees her again, though without meeting her or conversing with her. He looks at her through the window, underneath the 'huge moulded beams' of the house whose antiquity the narrator says did 'ponderously overhang a young wife who passed her time there…' As he looks, she enigmatically opens a work-box and looks tearfully at a photograph, whose we don't know, and then he leaves. The structure of the scene is repeated once again at the end of the next chapter which also ends with Sue indoors, Jude outside. The later scene stages and expresses again what has been noted above in this painful, unproductive, separated, and inconsequential interval which is Jude's wasted and tormented return to Sue's home. A gratuitous repetitive-ness without issue, an interval of baffled and pained feeling, an emotional drama of defeated comprehension and failed com-munication which returns the characters to their enigmatic singularity, and the desire to link—these things need no further comment.

A sense of these aspects of the text though can be deepened by an examination of the language of the extract. Here is its opening:

> He wandered about awhile, obtained something to eat; and then, having another half-hour on his hands, his feet involuntarily took him through the venerable graveyard of Trinity Church, with its avenues of limes, in the direction of the schools again. They were entirely in darkness. She had said she lived over the way at Old-Grove Place, a house which he soon discovered from her description of its antiquity...

This inconsequential episode seems to be just thought up on the spot by Hardy's narrator, as involuntarily as Jude's deciding to return in the direction of the schools again. The opening sentence seems to be filling in time, like Jude. Its terms are blurred, full of lassitude, its syntax anticipating nothing productive, 'He wandered about awhile, obtained something to eat'. However, a new initiative overtakes Jude and disrupts the sentence, breaking it into two halves separated by a semi-colon. Jude's behaviour seems obsessive, non-rational, driven, impulsive and mysterious. Such features contrast strongly with the 'avenues of limes' a phrase that could have come straight out of a George Eliot novel, where the planting of limes would suggest a productive linking of social and natural, past and future, a novelistic dedication to synthesis, that is wholly missing here. Moreover, the language threatens to break down:

> and then, having another half-hour on his hands, his feet involuntarily took him through the venerable graveyard of Trinity Church, with its avenues of limes, in the direction of the schools again. They were entirely in darkness.

The subject of this part of the sentence is the synecdoche, 'his feet'. It is these which are said to govern Jude, yet they themselves are said to do so 'involuntarily'. Moreover, next to each other we have the cliché 'on his hands' and the figure of 'his feet' so that literally we have a statement that says that Jude has time on his hands while his feet take him involuntarily. The language seems confused, threatening to dissolve Jude into a series of disconnected and incomprehensible body parts.

Similarly what do we make of the following short sentence 'They were entirely in darkness...'? Supposedly descriptive, description is overshadowed here by the impossibility of assigning reference to the pronoun. What or who does 'they' refer to? The context directs us to the schools or the trees, implicitly, though which we do not know, as we must be uncertain of a description of what is said to be 'entirely in darkness'. Further, the word 'they' should grammatically refer to the plural subject of the preceding sentence. Syntactically, then, it could be said to be Jude's feet which are entirely in darkness, as an aspect perhaps of their involuntary power over Jude. If one stops to meditate upon such matters one is troubled by the ways in which the word 'they' could refer to all these things, or even, symbolically, to Jude and Sue themselves, the suggestion of total darkness being an emblem of the irreducible obscurity which is their relationship. We can only reduce this attempted proliferation of meaning, here as throughout the novel, by intervening and wilfully forgetting and repressing its potentials of meaning, so consigning the moment of reading to the past.

What do we make of such features of the language of the text? In his study on cinema, Deleuze has written of how the frame as an informational system of the cinematic image can tend towards a reflexive emphasis on its own legible function, through a disruption of its own readability, achieved through saturation or rarefaction. Such an analysis is endlessly suggestive in terms of this passage, for the ways in which it is bent on disrupting narrative, and withholding information, while holding the reader and Jude within the unreadable present, where the lack of meaning coexists with the obduracy of language, its surplus potential. So too, the passage stages in many ways the activity of framing—through the brevity and self-contained compression of the scene itself; or again, through the use of frames within the scene—windows, photographs, the internal architecture of the living room with its overhanging beams. In terms of language, too, we have seen that an insistence on the means of expression goes along with a hollowing out of its informational function. As I have suggested, such a self-reflexivity in this text indicates not the masteries and continuities of consciousness and representation, but their powerlessness, their losses and divisions. Instead it provides merely the interpolated *mise en scène*, the testament of understanding's own defeat, and introversion.

Examples of this are many. When Jude sees the highway crossed by the now defunct 'ridge-way'[36] or Roman road, the junction implies a sense of the relativity and historicity of human forms and endeavour, a sense which includes the act of memory itself. As in *The Woodlanders*, the elegiac tonality of the narrative's recordings of place and community derives its full pathos from the prescient sense of their demise. Again one can mention Aunt's stale cakes and bread; the models of Jerusalem; the churches and colleges of Christminster; the photographs and artworks; the various references to religious doctrine, institutions and ceremonies; the narrator and Jude's allusions to scripture, music, architecture, art and literature; and finally, the constructions at Stoke-Barehills agricultural show, with its rows and rows of 'marquees, huts, booths, pavilions, arcades, porticoes—every kind of structure short of a permanent one...'[37]

This emphasis on the temporariness of things and the inevitable loss of the traces of memory defines, then, the spiralling introversion of a state of mind which remarks the obliteration of the mark which one had hoped to make upon the world, and which in turn anticipates the loss even of this consciousness:

> Before moving on he went and felt at the back of the stone for his own carving. It was still there; but nearly obliterated by moss...[38]

The accelerating sense of dissolution at the end of the novel, like a cinematic dissolve into an unseeable blankness, works through the self-destruction of novelistic norms of representation within the text. I have mentioned some of these things— the deaths of the children; the bizarre, parodic passion of Jude's death; the *deus ex machina* introduction of Little Father Time; Sue's return to Phillotson, and what Jude terms her 'enslavement to forms';[39] Arabella's reversion from evangelicalism to pigginess and Jude; the repeated scenes at the fairs, at Sue's window and the schoolroom; the increasingly parodic and contractedly superficial nature of the characterization; and so on. These insistent devices of contrived over-emphasis and repetition do not simply dissolve to a significant extent the novel's illusion of reality but involve, in the discarding of the frame of socially legible meanings, an opening to unreflected action, to the future.

Further, in his text on cinema, Deleuze has written of how every frame has as its absolute aspect an out-of-field to which it cannot be visibly or legibly related, since it is in terms of this out-of-field that the closed system is incorporated into the unclosed whole of the universe and duration. The 'closed system opens on to a duration which is immanent to the whole universe, which is no longer a set and does not belong to the order of the visible…'[40] The whole is defined by the virtualities of becoming, which are neither seen nor known, yet real. This is a recurrent theme in Deleuze's work, and central to this discussion. The process of becoming is inscribed always from within by the purely virtual limits of a generative nothingness which is the ultimate destiny, as well as the condition of the actual.[41] A certain obscurity or modernity, then, is the interval which sustains and exceeds the hegemony of reading, of conceptual thought, and recognition. In terms of the out-of-field, Boundas glosses this:

> The outside is not another site, but rather an out-of-site that erodes and dissolves all other sites. Its logic, therefore, is like the logic of difference, provided that the latter is understood in its transcendental and not in its empirical dimension: instead of difference between x and y, we must now conceive the difference of x from itself. Like the structure of supplementarity, whose logic it follows, the outside is never exhausted, every attempt to capture it generates an excess or a supplement that in turn feeds anew the flows of deterritorialisation, and releases new lines of flight.[42]

> [T]he Whole that is the Open—not the frame of all frames, but the unseen and the unrepresented that links frames together at the same time that it separates and differentiates them…[43]

Deleuze sees the relation to this absolute aspect of the out-of-field as an opening of the image onto the temporal and the spiritual:

> The more the image is spatially closed, even reduced to two dimensions, the greater is its capacity to *open itself* on to a fourth dimension which is time, and on to a fifth which is spirit…[44]

4 |

George Gissing—*The Odd Women*

The argument of this chapter is that it is not in its naturalism conceived as social documentation and polemic that Gissing's true and radical originality lies in *The Odd Women*, but in the text's delineation and expression of negative emotion. The discussion turns accordingly on noting, on the one hand, the scrupulous lucidity of Gissing's analyses of such states of feeling (and their causes and workings), while also noting, on the other hand, the diverse ways in which the text is itself gripped in its forms of expression by similarly powerful and solitary antipathies. So, the reader's affective experience of the novel is complex, at one with a participation in the systematic, if contradictory, recursiveness of a narrative that seems to offer itself simultaneously as *both* an animated critique and an enthralled symptom of a dehumanizing and isolating social world. For these reasons, the novel works as a text that passes on to the reader the affects of radical kinds of dissociation, as well as the insights of authorial consciousness. In the later part of the chapter, the ambivalent nature of Gissing's feminism is taken up more fully in relation to these emphases.

'I Am Not Suited for Society'

In picking out his intellectual powers as an enduring fascination of his work, Virginia Woolf also suggested that the reader of Gissing has the disconcerting impression that such a capacity for analysis itself proceeds from a condition of isolation which is endlessly repeated in his writing. The viewpoint of the text functions to draw the reader into the all-enclosing consciousness of the narrator ('[f]or Gissing is one of those imperfect novelists through whose books one sees the life of the author faintly covered by the lives of fictitious people...'):[1]

> We know Gissing as we do not know Hardy or George Eliot.
> Where the great novelist flows in and out of his characters and
> bathes them in an element which seems to be common to us all,
> Gissing remains solitary, self-centred, apart...[2]

In line with this, this chapter concentrates on the affects of
singleness and singularity—the two interlinked aspects of oddness—which distinguish Gissing's writing in *The Odd Women*.
Within the novel there is a tracing of asocial psychological
habits to their social conditions, revealing the disparity between these tendencies and society's recognizable images or
explanations of human motivation and relatedness (marriage,
romance, family life, and even political idealism). Gissing's
perennial involvement with the unregarded inhabitants of society's twilight zones, here with the superfluous women of the
1890s, enlivens accordingly an unremitting political critique on
behalf of single women, one which is driven not only by his
formidable critical intelligence, but also by powers of indignation which unleash a kind of violence against socially amelioris-
tic images of community. Gissing strips off the recognizable
mask of a human face which society assumes, to betray the
exorbitant forces and injustices which its norms are seen to
disguise. However, as this might suggest, by the same token this
questioning of society's assumed humanity proceeds from a
narrative perspective whose recognizable sympathies with the
disaffected seem also powerless to generate any countervailing
meaningful image or ideal of human relations. This is a fact
which often lends a productively qualified air to critical discussion of the novel's ostensible political concerns, as in John
Goode's comment, in what is the shrewdest and most dis-
cerning of accounts:

> ...despite its political centre *The Odd Women* remains a novel
> about isolation and rejection. The pairings which dominate the
> plot are both failures—neither of them can overcome the isolat-
> ing needs of their protagonists...[3]

This is a part of Goode's broader argument here as to how
Gissing's text dramatizes lives which are irreducibly incommu-
nicating, since he 'establishes oddness as a social characteristic,

like exile, like writing, which yokes together different lives
without constituting a community'.[4]

These features of the fiction define the critical task, then, as
in important part a need to account for the dispiriting division
in the fiction between its political elements, and the lack of
political potential within the world that is represented. But, as
suggested, things are more complicated than this, in that the
hostility which energizes the text's social criticism also is at
work ambivalently in the portrayal of society's victims. One
can consider here Harrison's response to the ambivalences of
the young Gissing who tutored his children, as described by
Korg:

> To Harrison, who was accustomed to dealing with practical
> matters, Gissing seemed to lack an ethical sense. He despised
> the ignorance and brutality of the poor whose way of life he had
> so vividly captured in his novel, and he wrote about them, it
> seemed to Harrison, simply to feed the pessimism he perversely
> enjoyed...[5]

This sense of a disparity—that Gissing's fiction employs, for
instance, modes of writing which can seem antipathetic to the
victims on whose behalf the text is ostensibly working—also
often marks critical discussions of Gissing's work. David Gryllis,
for instance, offers an accurate formulation of its problematic
nature at the beginning of his book, *The Paradox of Gissing*:

> George Gissing was a highly cultivated man who lived for
> many years in squalor and poverty, an aesthete who was also a
> social critic, a classicist obsessed with contemporary life. His
> attitude towards the proletarian poor was a peculiar compound of
> contempt and compassion, just as his appraisal of the upper class-
> es wavered between envy and impatient disdain...women he
> both idealized and despised...[6]

And, in line with this last comment, and with reference to the
feminism of *The Odd Women*, Alice B. Markow asks:

> Yet the question is this: was he an advocate of women's rights or
> a critic and provocateur? Most Gissing critics have observed the
> author's ambivalence and inconsistency regarding women.
> A few critics, such as Patricia Stubbs, Lloyd Fernando, Elaine
> Showalter and John Goode tend to regard Gissing as more or less
> supporting the ideal of the traditional woman, at least in his later

work. Still, most critics—Jacob Korg, Paul Sporn, Irving Howe, Carol Munn, Alison Cotes, Jean Kennard, Robert Selig, and Katherine Linehan, to name a few—do view Gissing as essentially feminist...[7]

Although it is important to probe these ambivalences in relation to women, it is not difficult to multiply examples of the intensities of Gissing's misogyny, for instance, in his study of Dickens where he praises the author for the 'fidelity to life' of his 'gallery of foolish, ridiculous, or offensive women',[8] or in a letter to Edward Bertz, where he wrote of how 'I am driven frantic by the crass imbecility of the typical woman'.[9]

In these, and in other ways, reading *The Odd Women* remains a radically discomfiting experience. The writing restlessly circulates between diverse and seemingly incompatible attitudes and affects. Nonetheless, it is striking how Gissing's writing attains through these fractured features strange powers and subtleties, particularly in its grimly fascinated enumeration of the dissociated and spasmodic intensities which play within and between the characters. As a way into this area, in this exchange between Monica and Widdowson the uneasy domestic tension is overturned by his expressions of jealousy and abjection:

> He had risen and was crushing her in his arms, his hot breath on her neck, when he began to whisper,—
>
> 'I want to keep you all to myself. I don't like these people—they think so differently—they put such hateful ideas into your mind—they are not the right kind of friends for you...'
>
> 'You misunderstand them, and you don't in the least understand me. Oh, you hurt me, Edmund!'
>
> He released her body, and took her head between his hands.
>
> 'I had rather you were dead than that you should cease to love me! You shall go to see her; I won't say a word against it. But, Monica, be faithful, be faithful to me!'
>
> 'Faithful to you?' she echoed in astonishment. 'What have I said or done to put you in such a state? Because I wish to make a few friends as all women do...'
>
> 'It's because I have lived so much alone. I have never had more than one or two friends, and I am absurdly jealous when you want to get away from me and amuse yourself with strangers. I can't talk to such people. I am not suited for society...'[10]

At this moment, as Widdowson's innermost emotions burst their banks, this dialogue also conveys to the reader that the differences between the characters are irresolvable. Their words have no genuine communicative function, merely reiterating a self-defensive assertiveness that in Widdowson's case assumes a murderous intensity. Accordingly, the reader's response divides itself and circulates between the partitioned worlds of the characters, so that the text becomes a remarkable traversing of separateness, and of the multiplex complications of the marital force field, the narrative catching what passes between the characters with its own kind of reversible double-sidedness. So powerfully, for instance, has the narrative conveyed Widdowson's frustration that a kind of subterranean involvement within his violence is unmistakeable, even as this yields instantaneously to a sense of Monica's repulsion ('his hot breath on her neck') and then to pity for him. And in between this we feel sympathy also for Monica, even primarily for her in her bemused and impossible position, caught as she is by the language of fidelity in an inhuman trap.

In such scenes, then, the narrative settles out as both a meticulous dissection and an expression of the affects which play between the tyrant and slave in the marital situation. It diagnoses the interplay between the characters in a way whose flexibility and clarity is extraordinary. Often phrase by phrase, the text catches and conveys the resonances and shocks of response and counter-response between the characters' uncommunicating worlds, occupying a kind of interspace between them in which the dynamics of the situation can be raised to expression. Within each character, too, there are repetitive circuits of incompatible and self-confounding emotion. So above, Widdowson's love seems indissociable from the deeper destructive workings of jealousy and a suffocating possessiveness. Again, Monica's attempt to find autonomy through marriage has led her to this incarceration, which leads her in turn to romantic fiction, and then ultimately to her rash, and even fateful, attempt to escape through her relation with Bevis.

In such ways, there is a real exploration of unconscious feeling in Gissing's writing which defines the text's problematic and disjunctive status. The term 'unconscious' is used in this connection to refer to these incapacitating habits of emotion which, as above, interrupt and control a consciousness which can reflect on them even as it cannot escape them. In what follows, the main thread will be the way in which Gissing's novel is a kind of experiment which traces these asocial forces and habits of dissociation at work in the minds of the characters. Further, in ways yet to to be fully described, through its language and formal features it works also itself to release and intensify such affects of dissociation, of *ressentiment* or jealousy, so that the reader comes both to observe and participate in these feelings. In the novel, for reader, character or narrator, positive human feelings appear to have been displaced by, or to mask, the most rudimentary obsessive gnawings, while these coexist—apparently in a kind of internal relation—with highly developed intellectual attitudes which turn back to study them even as they are caught up in repeating them. For the reader, this feature of Gissing's writing means that the encounter with the fiction is fundamentally a matter of the experience and contemplation of sensation and feeling, before it is a matter of social analysis. Discussing the ways in which it is customary to describe affective states, in *What is Philosophy?*, Deleuze and Guattari make some remarks which are useful here, paraphrasing Bergson:

> ...one has the impression that opinion misjudges affective states and groups them together or separates them wrongly...[11]

They continue with examples of fictional writers whose fictional works are monuments (in the ways discussed in Chapter 2 above) to the invention of affects which defeat custom and opinion, and which engender new contemplations of feeling. The prose of such writers preserves and provokes the sensations which release affects, ways of becoming, for the characters. Outside their recognizable selves the characters pass into new or unconsidered affective states, as with Zola's remorseless characters, or as with Proust, whose Swann and Marcel find the truth and meaning of love in the signs of jealousy:

> When Proust seems to be describing jealousy in such minute detail, he is inventing an affect, because he constantly reverses the order in affections presupposed by opinion, according to which jealousy would be an unhappy consequence of love; for

> him, on the contrary, jealousy is finality, destination; and if we
> must love, it is so that we can be jealous, jealousy being the
> meaning of signs—affect as semiology...[12]

In the last analysis, as far as *The Odd Women* is concerned, the
narrative can then appear as both a kind of contemplation and
a symptom of the powers of abjection and hatred.

'There Came an Interruption, Hurried, Peremptory...'

Of the many forms of dissociation (personal, social, familial,
marital, psychological) by which Gissing's *The Odd Women* is
possessed, death appears as the ultimate and recurrent manifestation. Death in this novel, however, is not only peculiarly
prevalent but of a peculiar and telling kind. In particular, death
is represented, in nearly all cases in the text, as obscurely just,
as a matter of individual responsibility or inadequacy. Typically, it appears as having been brought on by some fatal flaw,
weakness, or oversight, or by a suicidal impulse. Accordingly,
death seems less an interruption of a life than the fullest repetition of its incompletion or failure. Further, it appears all the
more sad the more appropriate it seems, the more it appears as
an expression of a denial of life or an incapacity for it.

Nevertheless, it is important here to distinguish those cases
which evoke a kind of mournfulness (such as Gertrude's death
by consumption, or the melancholic Isabella's suicide) from
those cases (such as Martha's death in the overturned pleasure-
boat), which seem to push a more ominous moral, implying
that a seeking of pleasure or distraction is incompatible with
the rigours of existence. There is a form of *ressentiment* here
which is important, and which recalls some points of Fredric
Jameson's discussion of *ressentiment* in Gissing's fiction, in
Chapter 4 of *The Political Unconscious*.[13] In Deleuze's analyses of
Nietzsche, *ressentiment* is, perhaps firstly, as has been said
earlier, a kind of recoil into memory brought about by an
excess of feeling, where the forgetting that sustains the unconscious actions and reactions of the body is interrupted. As
Deleuze says,

> As a result of his type the man of *ressentiment* does not 'react': his
> reaction is endless, it is felt instead of being acted...[14]

To take one implication of this: the type of *ressentiment*, then, can be seen as involving a failure of feeling (and a feeling of failure) that involves, as in Nietzsche's analyses, a compensating and contaminated moralism. The man of *ressentiment* turns censoriously and enviously against the irresponsibilities of more unreflective kinds of interaction, as a function of the confinement of his subjected and excessively memory-stricken consciousness in a kind of suspense and unhealthy passivity. In Gissing's text, such an attitude of narrative *ressentiment* can be discerned in the ways in which the text conveys, as with Martha's death, that it is the failure of representing one's responsibilities before an unyielding reality that is reprehensible or inadequate. The mere forgetful pursuit of the pleasures of the moment is an occupation prey to fatal disruptions. Once again, it is a moral of this kind that hovers over Dr Madden's death in the first chapter, after he (as Gissing's own father often did) had been reading Tennyson aloud to his family.[15] He dies because he had, typically, not taken the precaution of replacing his weak old horse, so that as 'in other matters...in this, postponement became fatality...'[16] The wilful and dreamy dissociation from necessary tasks and discomfiting future possibilities, which marks the doctor's practical dealings, becomes figured in his death, thrown from his cart, with a narrative irony which typically combines pathos with a certain humour at odds with it. The ironic narrative attitude here, for instance, seems to double an accentuated and consuming sense of the pitiable with a less overt but discernible sense of satisfaction in the appropriateness of disaster, and its shattering of the momentary effects of reciprocity and pleasure:

> Alice brought the volume and he selected 'The Lotus-Eaters'. The girls grouped themselves about him, delighted to listen. Many an hour of summer evening had they thus spent, none more peaceful than the present. The reader's cadenced voice blended with the song of the thrush:
>
>> '"Let us alone. Time driveth onward fast.
>> And in a little while our lips are dumb.
>> Let us alone. What is it that will last?
>> All things are taken from us..."'

> There came an interruption, hurried, peremptory...the doctor
> must come at once...[17]

Throughout the opening chapter there is a sense of the common experience of natural exteriority about to be lost—outside on the coast-down before the blue channel and the Welsh hills, or in the garden here, after an afternoon in 'the magnificent summer sunshine, and...western breeze that tasted of ocean' and that 'heightened his natural cheeriness...'[18] If in such examples the narrative invokes the harmonious capacities and horizons of nature and family, it seems above all as an occasion for their ironic eclipse. So, too, the common familial bonds, links involving place, finance, conversation, youth and poetry which are evoked, are set up only to be broken and lost after the interruption of the doctor's death, which takes place in the interval between the first chapter and the second chapter. In such ways the narrative draws the reader determinedly in the second chapter into a sense of the pathos of Alice and Virginia's life, of their pitiable refinement which mourns a sense of the lost poetry of existence. Nonetheless, the narrative also seems to relish on some obscure level the condition and actuality of their now prosaic drifting, fifteen years later, impecunious, fatigued, worn and anxious, in an utterly alien urban world.

There is, first, then, a kind of dramatization here of the conditions of *ressentiment*, in the interruptions of spontaneous affective relations, and the precipitation of the surviving Madden sisters into an ugly, overwhelmingly inhospitable reality. From this the recoil into problematic forms of introversion appears inevitable. Secondly, however, *ressentiment* appears an inner mainspring for the narrative's own powers of analysis and feeling. In terms of the narrative attitude, sympathy, or at least an accentuated sense of the pitiable, is inseparable from an unfeeling, poised attitude which takes a kind of intellectual satisfaction in registering and demonstrating implacably, as if by a syllogism, the truth of a character's fate and misfortune. Gissing's text is animated by this complex double-sidedness, a characteristic combination of boundless pathos and merciless irony. This is evident in the striking treatment of Alice and Virginia which draws comfort from their destitution, as was already suggested in the representation of the dead mother of the first chapter, with her 'secret anxieties'.[19] To attempt a general statement here, it is simply the case that there is operative in Gissing's fiction an obscure economy of feeling whereby to feel for another person seems only possible where that person is necessarily reduced to unhappiness, and so converted into a kind of uncommunicating state of pitiable powerlessness and abject isolation. Conversely, happiness or pleasure as to do with animated human reciprocity is resented. It appears as an idyll of memory or fantasy, a facile expression of vanity, or of a dangerously heedless obliviousness. Pity and irony are the mutually implicated if divergent means, then, whereby in Gissing's fiction the text's contradictory affective and analytic attitudes make up a complex narrative system of thought and feeling at the level of expression.

It is further testimony to Gissing's analytic powers that the text probes such ambivalences and their implications with a peculiar clarity in the world it constructs. As an aspect of this, it is striking how little, for instance, even Rhoda's feminism can seem at times to have to do with compassion and fellow-feeling. Her rational attitude of pragmatism, as a clear-eyed recognition of the bleak exigencies of social conditions, and of the need to intervene only where it is possible to make a difference, is admirably lucid and rigorous. However, it is also at times a seemingly intractable kind of attitude which can express itself with an unsparing relish, as, for instance, when she sympathizes with Barfoot's temptation to whip his sister-in-law, or when she says to Monica that her aim is 'to make women hard-hearted'.[20] Above all, she values a militant form of ethical and political discipline, as when she and Mary debate whether they should take in Bella Royston again, after her affair with a married man:

> ...one of the supreme social needs of our day is the education of women in self-respect and self-restraint. There are plenty of people—men chiefly, but a few women also of a certain temperament—who cry for a reckless individualism in these matters. They would tell you that she behaved laudably, that she was *living out herself*—and things of that kind. But I didn't think you shared such views...[21]

Rhoda's resistance to Mary's sympathy is in one way a wholly

justifiable concomitant of her pragmatism, and it is this single-
mindedness that is so impressive in her characterization. However, there are times when this can also involve the assumption
of disturbingly rigid and unfeeling traits, as indicated even
more clearly by the rhetorical image she uses when talking to
Monica of female misery:

> '... I wish girls fell down and died of hunger in the streets,
> instead of creeping to their garrets and the hospitals. I should
> like to see their dead bodies collected together in some open
> place for the crowd to stare at.'
>
> Monica gazed at her with wide eyes.
>
> 'You mean, I suppose, that people would try to reform things.'
>
> 'Who knows? Perhaps they might only congratulate each
> other that a few of the superfluous females had been struck
> off...'[22]

Oddity

Henry James's dictum that fiction requires the 'oxygen of possibility' is often cited by Deleuze as a principle of fiction that
touches on a philosophical theory of the Other Person.[23] Accordingly, the characteristics of James's style—its circumspection and obliquity—become the means by which a narrative
method can elaborate the social and dramatic workings of
viewpoint, probing, with access to a privileged consciousness,
the recesses of minds which are necessarily interdependent but
capable of all kinds of privacy and difference. James's texts are
true to the equivocal mysteries of the expressions of other
possible worlds which are given by other people's actions,
manners and words. In Deleuze's terms, this structured difference, of the perceptual worlds of others within the field of my
perception, defines subjective experience as essentially oriented in terms of others, as a movement and process of learning, if
not of knowledge. James's texts aspire accordingly to reproduce
in their language the inexhaustible, provisional, and endlessly
self-renewing nature of human relatedness.[24] In Gissing's fiction,
differently, the scrupulous multiplication and realization of
distinct viewpoints is in its way equally remarkable. However,
these are minds that are in important ways commonly
concerned to preserve a troubled sense of autonomy through a

reduction or extinguishing of the separate mystery of other people. As this might suggest, there is a perverse and self-contradictory logic at work here which is unfolded time and again in *The Odd Women*. Importantly, it results in a development of the portrayal of human psychology beyond the surface manifestations of *ressentiment* into a portrayal of its most radical and diabolic, if commonplace, forms. So, for example, in the main love stories of the text, as in the example above, love can appear a mask behind which we discern a destructive machinery of pure self-assertion, interpersonal accusation or panic, systematic non-understanding, and unregarding and absolute kinds of possessiveness and jealousy.

Most straightforwardly, then, in these ways Gissing's text traces the cruel logic whereby a pitiable condition of exclusion and estrangement becomes confirmed as a psychological predicament. In this sense, oddity derives from personal fixations, eccentricities, fantasies or obsessions which enclose someone more determinedly than any jailor within their own exclusive world. Rhoda's sense of mission, Alice's brand of Christianity, Isabella's suicide, Bella's suicide, even Mrs Barfoot's passion for Everard are obvious instances of this. Gissing's title, and his novel, explores the plight of women and the relation between the sexes in terms of these notions of the singular and the single mentioned above, these two aspects of oddness.

Consider, as an obvious example of these things, the text's remarkable presentation of Virginia, her fixation with poor fiction, and the gradual decline into an alcoholism that separates her from everyone around her. She drinks because she is lonely, but drink makes her more lonely and prevents her from overcoming her situation. Alone the virgin Virginia turns in an escapist fashion to gin, and makes virginity inescapable. Gissing is a connoisseur of such miseries, unceasing in his exploration of the internal repetitions by which psychology appeases and responds to the sense of abandonment, manifesting its own kinds of counter-rejection of the social rejection which is suffered. Here the narrator draws the reader into the emotional poverty and unfulfilment of the characters and into the unconscious anger involved which often takes the forms of guilt or fantasy, or depression, or addiction to intoxication. The text charts the

variety and nature of all sorts of psychological traps, hamster
wheels and loops of loneliness, with a sort of inexorable bleak-
ness. It presents the interior responses to social exclusion as the
means often of exacerbating, in a correlative and even more
insidious way, the kinds of powerlessness and isolation to which
they were responses. In this way the text represents singleness
as a condition that can intensify through the singularity that
results from attempts to compensate. The text demonstrates
this ghastly interior logic with a typical mixture of cold humour, and pity (something diabolic and gloating in the humour,
something prostrated and abandoned in the pity, as if the
pitied person were a surrogate self). Because Virginia has no
one to speak to about the depth of her feelings of destitution,
she indulges in something that is unspeakable. As this example
suggests also, there is a silence here which is part circumstantial
and part social in Virginia's case. Silence is the precondition of
Virginia's situation and her recourse to drink and fiction. But
again, through these forms of escape, a psychological silence,
all the more oppressive and unbreakable, results. Similarly with
Rhoda, her solitude becomes isolation when her feeling for
Barfoot divides her from Mary, and from herself and her work,
precipitating her into a struggle for mastery. This linking, then,
of singleness and singularity, of exclusion and uncountenanced
dimensions of unconscious feeling and behaviour, can be seen
throughout the text. I have mentioned Monica's attempt to find
independence through marriage, and then to find love through
Bevis, a narrowing obsession that results in her death. Again,
one could discuss here the presentation of Everard's Amy, or
Miss Royston. These are women who seem destined for a long
slide that is in part conditioned by social means and in part by
internal responses.

   Beyond all this, the inner logic of such psychological predica-
ments, and of the effects of loneliness, is detectable in the novel
in ways that make it of consuming interest. Put concisely, and
to generalize what I have suggested about Virginia, the novel
explores how isolation and dissociation is the condition of all
kinds of psychological negativity and reproach which reproduce the lack of relatedness which is inscribed in the initial
situation. I have used *ressentiment* as a kind of fundamental

schema to begin to describe the text's explorations of a psychic fate of repetition and dissociation expressed in many connected forms (depression, jealousy, possessiveness, suicide, hatred, the desire for power, self-pity, resentment, insecurity), inner states of negativity whose grim mechanics and double-binds Gissing's novel explores. These are forms of behaviour in which the determined attempt to escape a psychological predicament of loneliness becomes the means of indirectly expressing and perpetuating it. Within *ressentiment*, then, there is also a kind of living protest, and the repetition of a thwarted potential at odds with the stultified aspects of its conscious contents or concomitants, a seed of health that is bound to a mode of destruction.[25]

The perversity of the resulting attitudes are explicable here, then, only because what is insistent in the self-defeating behaviour is an expression of reproach and anger, of a feeling of injustice. A sense of wrong and silence repeats and recalls itself, in a form which cannot be countenanced or heard within society's norms. To take one of the men as a further example of Gissing's presentation of alienation, the remarkable presentation of Widdowson's obsessive jealousy is an attempt to overcome loneliness through the incarceration of the beloved, to overcome a distance and a separation from Monica that merely confirms it and makes it absolute. Jealousy, indeed, is a central and essential form of *ressentiment* in this text, as in Rhoda's feeling for Everard. Jealousy seeks to appease singleness by an obsessive regard, an obviously self-defeating singularity that ultimately betrays its ironic structure by tending to lead to the demise of the relationship it sought to protect. (If the aim of jealousy is indeed to protect a relation and not unconsciously to dissever it.) So, in *The Odd Women*, separation between people, even within relationships, is presented as the order of things.

In *Proust and Signs*, Deleuze discusses jealousy in terms that are applicable here.[26] The jealous lover hungers after the beloved's signs of preference. However, these safeguards against the fear of being discarded are also indexes of an alien, autonomous and sovereign world, enveloped in the beloved and expressed in these very signs. In this world, one is merely one among many potentially transitory persons or phenomena (and the jealous attitude fears a repetition of the sense of interrupted affectivity which repeats itself as jealousy). Deception, exclusion and uncertainty define the affect of jealousy as the truth of love:

> Indeed, it is inevitable that the signs of a loved person, once we 'explicate' them, should be revealed as deceptive; addressed to us, applied to us, they nonetheless express worlds which exclude us and which the beloved will not and cannot make us know... Love's signs...are deceptive signs which can be addressed to us only by concealing what they express: the origin of unknown worlds, of unknown actions and thoughts which give them a meaning...[27]

Jealousy is, for Proust, according to Deleuze, a dissociative structure which eventually expresses itself at the end of a relationship as that to which love tends in principle. The joy of inclusion, in the loved one's world, relieves only a more fundamental exclusion and dependence. The pain of dispensability always inhabits the pleasures of love. Here this can be clearly accounted for because dissociation has always been the principle, now realized, operating between the two people, in so far as each is unknown to the other. Accordingly, the lover comes to a kind of freedom, and a kind of hateful joy, as he discovers the truth that his love is separable from the person who was, contingently, its target. The lover now can understand that his loves are a series of repetitious expressions of an idea that can never be identified with, or exhausted by, the individualwith whom it is associated in fact. In this way, Deleuze's discussion articulates as intrinsic to the structure of jealous love a lack of belief in reciprocity and a condition of dissociation which bear on the version of Gissing developed here.

So, in one respect, one can see in *The Odd Women* how the jealous lover, as in Widdowson's dealings with Monica, at once operates with deception himself, and assumes it on the part of the other. In the process he destroys the intimacy he is attempting to preserve, by virtue of the paradoxical means he is employing—secrecy, silence, distrust, spying, incarceration, resentment, humiliation of himself and her. No relationship in the text escapes these features and appears satisfactory. The relationships are non-relationships in the last analysis, charting the divisions and emotional impotence, the jealousy and solipsistic machinery which recur in each and every case. Beyond the social critique which offers an ostensible condition for these things, the text uncovers deeper human inadequacies with its own kind of intensity and inevitability. The law of Gissing's text is that the attempt to compensate for the abuses of law leads to an enthralment every bit as absolute, and far more disquieting; the unconscious can constitute a more pitiless and remorseless, because habitual and demoralizing, machinery of oppression than that of social norms.

However, it can be argued that as well as offering a critique of the blindnesses and exclusions, the double-binds and silencings, which are presented as the ultimate truths of social forms and of love, the text also demonstrates more positive human attributes and possibilities. After all, the discussion above notwithstanding, Rhoda is a character capable of renouncing her own happiness in relation to a wider view, and it is in the depth and tension of the presentation of these aspects of her life that the text works most fully. Rhoda is presented so sympathetically that her renunciation seems all the more compelling. Yet even here the most cursory discussion of her feelings for Barfoot cannot disguise the unconscious aspect in which their relationship is a struggle for power and dominance, as much as a meeting of minds and bodies. A kind of savage self-assertion and blindness to the other, at least as absolute as that of Widdowson, can be discerned here, to suggest that Rhoda even remains as much a victim of psychological determinism, an oppressed consciousness seeking a compensatory self-aggrandizement, as any of the other characters:

> The interest would only be that of comedy. She did not love Everard Barfoot, and saw no likelihood of ever doing so; on the whole, a subject of thankfulness. Nor could he seriously anticipate an assent to his proposal for a free union; in declaring that legal marriage was out of the question for him, he had removed his love-making to the region of mere ideal sentiment. But, if he loved her, these theories would sooner of later be swept aside; he would plead with her to become his legal wife.
>
> To that point she desired to bring him. Offer what he might, she would not accept it; but the secret chagrin that was upon her

would be removed. Love would no longer be the privilege of other women. To reject a lover in so many respects desirable, who so many women might envy her, would fortify her self-esteem, and enable her to go forward in the chosen path with firmer tread...[28]

The subtlety and shading of Gissing's writing in such passages, the amount of psychological implication, is remarkable, and it may be that this presenting of the seething unconscious forces which offer another kind of oppression is Gissing's most remarkable characteristic. In Gissing's world, then, subjectivity is constituted as subjection, between the twin forces of society and the unconscious, and it is in the drawing out of the nature and logic of these interconnected forces that Gissing's text works most disquietingly.

'Architectural Fragments, Chiefly Dismembered Columns'

This section begins by examining the text's representation of the kinds of affective dysfunctioning which afflict the men in the novel, and relates this discussion of these habits of feeling to the narrative values of the text's language and organization. As a way into this area, here is the strange, disconnected paragraph which begins Chapter 5, where Monica's first arranged meeting with Widdowson takes place:

> At that corner of Battersea Park which is near Albert Bridge there has lain for more than twenty years a curious collection of architectural fragments, chiefly dismembered columns, spread in order upon the ground, and looking like portions of a razed temple. It is the colonnade of old Burlington House, conveyed hither from Piccadilly who knows why, and likely to rest here, the sporting ground for adventurous infants, until its origin is lost in the abyss of time...[29]

It is possible to read this passage as encompassing the widest symbolic references. Hence, the sense of a lost distinction and grandeur, or at least of a communal refinement now somewhat degraded and scarcely recognized in the urban world, is a note often struck in the text in its portrayal of the Madden family ('Yet Virginia could not have been judged anything but a lady...').[30] Dismembered, like the family of which Gissing's narrator gives the reader a relatively prelapsarian image in the first chapter, the fragments here too have been now rather arbitrarily, even mysteriously, relocated in an inhospitable setting ('who knows why'), and are subject also to all kinds of potential humiliations ('the sporting ground for adventurous infants') in their decline towards oblivion. Like the Madden family, the architectural portions occupy a strangely useless and painful between time, at odds with a world which has little function for them any more. Like Virginia or Alice, they anticipate, also, in varying degrees of derangement or fragmentation, the erasures of the 'abyss of time'.

However, it is further indicative of the ways in which this text works that the passage could equally be taken as anticipating the portrayal of Widdowson, and by extension, perhaps, the other male characters in the text. If Widdowson's formality of manner appears an arrangement designed to offset humiliation or ridicule, it is because it also testifies, in its petrified stiffness, to a certain disorganized affective functioning. And so, the loneliness to which he later confesses in this chapter appears not merely pitiable, but also as an index of a profound dissociation which in his marriage manifests itself threateningly as an unbounded emotional insecurity and a primal kind of possessiveness. Widdowson's demeanour disguises, then, not only the fragmentation of what society would see as his manhood, but also the infantile impulses which take possession of these ruins and play among them. The rational and moral workings of consciousness are insistently disrupted in such a way as testifies to the earliest affective sense of interruption, whose effects are still unconsciously operating. If this schema is applicable to Gissing's text, it is striking how the scene here suggests these things while also its form of writing suffers a kind of disruption. Such meanings seems to possess the text implicitly, as a kind of imploring and unarticulated power of potential meaning, behind all its explicit detail and syntactical articulation.

There is, then, here a sense of a disparity between the meticulously maintained specificities of the text's naturalistic surface, and the more repetitive attitudes or preoccupations which play beneath, and which tend to draw its detail into obsessional orbits. And so, few readers of Gissing will have escaped

a troubled sense that his texts combine in paradoxical and even
insidious ways a naturalistic representation with the play of
odd affects which come to control the reader's response in a
determined and often covert way at the same time. So, for the
reader, within a paragraph as seemingly inconsequential and
descriptive as the one above, the text conveys a general sense
of malaise, of indignation and powerlessness, of emotions which
are both fixated and chaotic. This is evident, also, in how beneath their surface distinctions the characters seem taken over
by the general form of a fate of *ressentiment*. So Widdowson's
personality seems not only to recall the collapsed and defunct
frontage of Burlington House, but also to be a kind of repetition of what we learn of his father in this same chapter:

> I'm afraid my father had a good many faults that made her life
> hard. He was of a violent temper, and of course the deafness
> didn't improve it. Well, one day a cab knocked him down in the
> King's Road, and from that injury, though not until a year after,
> he died... I was sent into the office of the man who had been
> my father's partner, to serve him and learn the business. I did
> serve him for years, and for next to no payment, but he taught
> me nothing more than he could help. He was one of those
> heartless, utterly selfish men that one meets too often in the
> business world...[31]

The kinds of repetition which govern the relationships here,
so that *ressentiment* perpetuates itself across society and the gen-
erations, is strikingly demonstrated in *The Odd Women*. In men
this takes the forms of violence, arrogance, ill will, infantilism,
misery, jealousy, and vanity, and of it Widdowson's father's
deafness seems an obviously appropriate image. With no real
exception, men are weak and fall short of necessary kinds of
human response. Widdowson, we have seen, alienates Monica
through his behaviour and is physically repellent; Barfoot
seems perversely to allow his relationship to Rhoda to floun-
der; Bevis is incapable of responding fully to Monica's needs,
and so on. This is a punitive kind of narrative demonstration,
then, in which men are represented in the text in terms of absolute kinds of egoism.

At the end of Chapter 26, Barfoot has left the disconsolate
Rhoda at Seascale, without attempting to correct her jealous
misapprehension about Monica:

At eight o'clock next morning Barfoot was seated in the south-
ward train. He rejoiced that his strength of will had thus far
asserted itself. Of final farewell to Rhoda he had no thought
whatsoever. Her curiosity would, of course, compel her to see
Monica...

Violent rain was beating upon the carriage windows; it drove
from the mountains, themselves invisible, though dense low
clouds marked their position. Poor Rhoda! She should not have a
very cheerful day at Seascale. Perhaps she would follow him by
a later train. Certain it was that she must be suffering intensely—and that certainly rejoiced him. The keener her suffering
the sooner her submission. Oh, but the submission should be
perfect! He had seen her in many moods, but not yet in the
anguish of broken pride. She must shed tears before him, declare
her spirit worn and subjugated by torment of jealousy and fear.
Then he would raise her, and seat her in the place of honour,
and fall down at her feet, and fill her soul with rapture.

Many times between Seascale and London he smiled in anticipation of that hour...[32]

Although this is the central romance of the novel, and Everard
even perhaps the most sympathetic male character, the passage
is possessed in all its aspects by vicious emotion. The language
and set-up of the scene indicate an emotional situation that
denies any natural kind of reciprocity, and that substitutes
obsessive and cruel manipulation for more positive emotion
and interchange. Everard gloats over the idea that his with-
drawal from the scene without farewell will lead Rhoda to
humiliate herself before Monica, and also ultimately, before
himself. Sadistic as Everard's motivation appears, however, it
also appears itself deeply determined, unconscious. The language of the passage suggests this self-dissociation even through
the first passive verb, 'At eight o'clock next morning Barfoot
was seated...' which suggests the compulsive nature of the
psychological rails along which he is being moved, and through
the odd locutions in the following sentence, 'He rejoiced that
his strength of will had thus far asserted itself...' Further, the
narrative in typical fashion here adapts itself to a form of inner
monologue, whose content centres on the absence of any human dialogue in the situation.

These psychological and emotional values which inform the
passage, then, reiterate kinds of dissociation which can be seen

in many other typical features of the passage. For instance, it is worth noting how the passage combines its syntactical units in a kind of series of little episodes, but without linkage, or development, or happy continuity. Each unit seems separated by a kind of interval from what follows, and specifies a moment or cell of intense and restless emotion, an all-consuming thought. The constricted and brooding attitude which is conveyed in this ruminative language does not develop outside the succession of interior moments given by the clauses. These follow one another with a certain grimly determined motion, and without any aesthetically pleasing form. Again the scene itself is psychologically expressive. The invisible natural beauty of the scene, the low dense clouds and the violent rain beating on the carriage windows, the determined progress of the train along its narrow rails—all these things have a deep inwardness with the affective parameters of Gissing's world here. Everard's talk of will and mastery seems a cover for the sense we get that the origin of his own emotions is not within his control. The hidden landscape and the rain beating violently against the interior of the carriage appear as a figure for the way his consciousness is shaken by obscure and unnatural emotion. As so often in the novel, the desire for self-assertion and subjugation of another appears as an attempt to compensate for one's own division and destitution before powerful unconscious forces.

One can connect such reiterative, disconnected and unchanging features with some larger structural features of the novel. As with the passage, one is struck by the way Gissing puts together his chapters serially, as it were, out of small scenes, each centring on a different aspect of an emotional situation, yet each reiterating the depressive values of the text. Similarly, in terms of the novel's portrayal of time: often we get a sense of the character's powerlessness as expressed through long intervals that have simply to be endured or wished away. The characters occupy their purely solitary emotional and mental orbits, as when Widdowson patrols outside Monica's lodgings, or when Rhoda attempts to kill time in the Lake District, or even when Barfoot goes abroad. Over and over again in the novel time is a kind of prison sentence to be endured. The characters inhabit an unmeaning interval, a period which is static and which most often corresponds to the characters' desire for a contact by which they can overcome their sense of isolation. Widdowson wishes and waits perpetually for Monica to be his. Rhoda waits for Everard to offer himself to her on terms that she can accept. Virginia passes an evening at home with her booze. Like the sleepless nights which so many of the characters pass, their repetitive preoccupations and restless nervousness disrupt the course of nature. Time goes forward but does not bring change or human meaning, or another person really to breach loneliness. Instead it constitutes merely a duration to be passively undergone. The only strong contrast to this is Micklethwaite's courtship, and eventual happy ending, which is put down to his labours towards making his marriage possible. However, this seems pasted on to the novel rather, as a half-hearted attempt to use sentimentality to distract us from the novel's almost universal pattern of non-relatedness.

As against the dramatization of this pattern in episodic structures of waiting and suspense, we can mention another negative aspect of time as it appears in the text. This is the time of the violent instant, of the purely destructive, ironic and catastrophic event which interrupts and destroys, and which is at once accidental and therefore pitiful, and yet also in some sense deserved. There are many further significant cases of this, including that of Monica who dies in childbirth.

Finally, it is possible to make some connections between these two kinds of time in the novel (that of passive expectation and that of surprise and disaster) and the analyses of temporality which Deleuze elaborates in his discussions of sadism and masochism in *Coldness and Cruelty*. At the heart of this essay Deleuze places again the notion of a transcendental synthesis of time itself, a pure form beyond and beneath the repetitions of past and present:

> It is at once repetition of before, during and after, that is to say it is a constitution in time of the past, the present and even the future. From a transcendental viewpoint, past, present and future are constituted in time simultaneously, even though, from the natural standpoint, there is between them a qualitative difference...[33]

Deleuze draws this out of Freud's discussion in *Beyond the Plea-sure Principle* of the death instinct as the transcendental foun-dation of psychic life. The universality of the pleasure principle in experience, of its binding repetitions constitutive of the present, of pleasure, and of emerging life, necessitates a more fundamental pure repetition, identified with the death instinct, Thanatos. A heterogeneous necessity, never evident as such in experience, it is nonetheless this ungrounded force of repeti-tive destruction and futurity that, on Deleuze's reading of Freud, grounds Eros as the condition of experience, and makes possible a future of conservation and loss. Repetition precedes the pleasure principle as its unconditioned condition, regard-less of the fact that within empirical experience repetition appears as subordinate to the operations of Eros. In a way suggestive for the study of Gissing's novel, destruction as the necessity of repetition emerges as the nonhuman hidden condi-tion of construction, production and reproduction. Without going further into the nuances and distinctions of Deleuze's discussion of the incommensurable pathologies of sadism and masochism, or trying to map Gissing's text onto that discussion, it is possible, nonetheless, to emphasize as relevant here the crucial common feature of Sacher-Masoch and Sade's work, for Deleuze. This lies in their invocation of the repetition of the pure eventual form of time in the dissolute and ungrounded dimension of Thanatos. Pain is not the source of sexual pleasure in either case, but is the result of a desexualization consequent upon the undoing of the binding of Eros. Sexual pleasure results instead from the resexualization of pure, separated repetition, Thanatos:

> Both sadism and masochism imply that a particular quantity of
> libidinal energy be neutralized, desexualized, displaced and put
> at the service of Thanatos...[34]

The difference here is that in the case of the sadist the superego expels from itself its ego, which is projected out onto the world, the victim and a secondary, maternal, nature, in an act of perverse identification resulting in the 'destructive madness' of a self-generating, intellectual, negation.[35] The wild delirium of this deranged idealism is itself merely the 'reflection of a

higher form of violence', resulting from an impersonal imperative attributable to an ideal institution of violence as an expression of a destructive primary nature.[36] In the case of the
masochist the superego is subject to a double disavowal—in the
merely apparent incarnation of the maternal tortures; and in
the essentially disguised figure of the father as superego in the
beaten victim. The superego can be disavowed because it
negates itself as contradictorily imagined in torturer and tor-
tured. In both cases, then, the death instinct is the common,
transcendental element, but masochism and sadism remain
essentially uncommunicating.

There are several implications which can be drawn from this
foreshortened digression for the discussion of Gissing. In the
first place, Deleuze's essay emphasizes that although there are
forms of sadism specific to masochism and vice versa, they
remain essentially wholly divergent symptoms of dissociation.
Accordingly, as Nicholas Blincoe has argued, the political idea
that would attempt to constitute a common space for the relations of master and slave is deeply problematic.[37] More specifically, it is possible to argue for a difference in kind within
Gissing's text: of a certain masochism evident in the suspended
and powerless imaginative intervals, in which many of the
characters exist as waiting, and for a certain sadism in the
interruptive and demonstrable violence of events which revenge themselves on the weaknesses of the characters, in so far
as they are either feminine, or in the case of the men, otherwise
lacking in a sufficient masculinity.

'She Had Ceased to Breathe'

At this point the supposed feminism of the text becomes a
more than questionable sort of category. For instance, it is a
remarkable (and apparently unremarked) feature of this text
that no mother survives it. Mrs Madden is dead on the first
page, Widdowson's mother is dead, Everard's mother is dead,
Micklethwaite's betrothed's mother is dead, and Monica dies at
the end. Alongside this, Isabel drowns herself, Gertrude and
Martha die, Mrs Hungerford dies, Bella Royston dies and so on.

One could relate this, as Gryllis does, to Gissing's own unhappiness at this time, though in fact his first child had just been born:

> The peak period of Gissing's antipathy to women occurred in the 1890s. Wretchedly unhappy in his marriage to Edith, he discharged his bile in a series of works, from *Born in Exile,* to his book on Dickens, which offers a crescendo of misogyny...[38]

Gryllis goes on in this connection to note the representation of Barfoot's friends' wives in the novel:

> one of his friends, whose wife lacked humour, has ended up in a lunatic asylum; another, whose helpmeet clacked incessantly of servants has become a pitiable nomad. Everard's own brother kowtows to a wife who is both a hypochondriac and a vulgar socialite...[39]

In these aspects of the novel, the unremitting scourging of men as lovers, and women as beloved, has a kind of repetitive intensity which seems at one with a kind of pitiless, punitive, impersonal strain in the text. It is as if these people were in some way victims of a perverse kind of revenge upon the possibility of love, the narrator taking a dark satisfaction in the sort of serial destruction of human love as a possibility. The different narrative lines in the text radiate out as repetitions of human dissociation and self-division. Some such working in the text may account for something of its baffled emotional atmosphere, its odd mixture of guilt and pathos, of energy and utter prostration of spirit, its depression and its grim satisfaction, its simultaneous tapping of the emotions of victim and tyrant, of Monica and Widdowson. After all, self-pity and self-laceration are ideas that can easily be reconciled where the division between victim and victimizer takes place within the same psyche. And as such forms of behaviour are at once means of escaping and confirming a psychological predicament and loneliness, so then they bear an internal relation to the norms which refuse to countenance such forms of behaviour. These would be forms of behaviour, then, construable as phrases in terms of a lost addressee, in which accusation, because of neglect (look what's become of me), and a self-defeating compensation are involved (I hate you, and to punish you I will destroy my own social identity). As this suggests,

Gissing's novel is fundamentally about psychological isolation and the perverse imperatives which result. A self-punishing interpersonal logic is duplicated within the self, as the means of sustaining an ambivalent relation to the lost, resented, familial and social contexts and actants from which the emotional habits derive. These are contexts, accordingly, whose norms have all kinds of contradictory, perverted, deferred and remote effects within the psychological torture chamber which the characters inhabit. Finally here, with reference to the points above, it is possible to see much of the reproachful unhappiness in the text, with its odd combination of diabolic protest and dispirited forlorn loneliness, as fixated habits referrable to, or directed at, the figure of the missing or dead mother.

Because of these characteristic complexities of expression and content, the political critique of Gissing's text cannot engender a compensating faith in social and human relations, or sociohistorical development. In its workings the novel is both a profound exploration and an expression of affective states which are in their nature introverted and anti-rational, and from which neither the narrator nor any of the characters are genuinely immune. So human differences and desires, as in the love and familial stories of the text, appear necessarily unnegotiable in the last analysis. Affective relations of power and control merely work to bind together the uncommunicating and inimical solitudes of the characters. Further, as has been argued, Gissing's ostensible sympathetic involvements—with the victim, and with the feminism of Mary and Rhoda—can accordingly be seen as a kind of cover for both the exploration and expression of affects which are less recognizable or more perplexing. These are identifications which can seem also ultimately the disguises for the exercise of an underground hostility and relish. The text has it both ways, raising a piteous protest on behalf of those who suffer from the prosaic anxieties and undeflected miseries of the novel's nether world, while also working in its forms of expression powerfully against any instantiation of human communication as a social or emotional possibility.

In these respects, Gissing is here seen, then, as pre-eminently an analyst of the sad passions of isolation and dissociation—a dramatist of the conditions of these ways of relating, as well as of their deficiencies and paradoxical kinds of working and satisfaction. Moreover, in its working his fiction makes these affects inescapable for the reader. As an aspect of this, syntax and paragraph take on an accumulative rhythm of neurotic disquiet whose joyless, enumerative, meditations are the expressions of a self-communing attitude which recognizes natural beauty, but as if in impossible weather, and the possibility of love, but as if from a point of irreducible exile. Above all, for all the text's identification with the plight of women, its identification extends ultimately only to their undoing. The paradox here between an identification with the victim and with the victimizer can be unfolded from the schema of *ressentiment* which repeats as the narrative of a resentful life the affective dissociation it presupposes.

5 |

Joseph Conrad—*The Shadow-Line*

In his author's note to *The Shadow-Line*, Conrad makes explicit his disavowal of any intention in the tale to 'touch on the supernatural', a disavowal that preserves the truly sensible mysteries of nature:

> But I could never have attempted such a thing, because all my moral and intellectual being is penetrated by an invincible conviction that whatever falls under the dominion of our senses must be in nature and, however exceptional, cannot differ in its essence from all the other effects of the visible and tangible world of which we are a self-conscious part. The world of the living contains enough marvels and mysteries as it is; marvels and mysteries acting upon our emotions and intelligence in ways so inexplicable that it would almost justify the conception of life as an enchanted state...[1]

The visible and tangible materiality of the world includes self-consciousness as an effect which is powerless to explain the true 'marvels and mysteries of life'. Such things are thinkable only when nature is conceived as excluding dimensions transcendent to it:

> No, I am too firm in my consciousness of the marvellous to be ever fascinated by the mere supernatural, which (take it any way you like) is but a manufactured article, the fabrication of minds insensitive to the intimate delicacies of our relation to the dead and to the living, in their countless multitudes; a desecration of our tenderest memories; an outrage on our dignity...[2]

Further, the belief in transcendent worlds of the spirit is seen to be an illusion crudely hostile to the workings of human sensitivity and dignity, which are, above all, a matter of 'our relation to the dead and the living', a matter of sympathy.

Indeed, 'sympathy' is not only perhaps the most important idea in Conrad's *The Shadow-Line*, but also in an equally important sense the motive behind the writing of the text. The Author's Note to Conrad's *The Shadow-Line* famously, if also reticently, makes explicit (as does the text's dedication 'To Borys and All Others') his desire at the time of writing to express a continuity between the experiences of his youth, and those of his son, who in 1916 was involved in the war:

> Primarily the aim of this piece of writing was the presentation of certain facts which certainly were associated with the change from youth, care-free and fervent, to the more self-conscious and poignant period of maturer life. Nobody can doubt that before the supreme trial of a whole generation I had an acute consciousness of the minute and insignificant character of my own obscure experience. There could be no question here of any parallelism. That notion never entered my head. But there was a feeling of identity, though with an enormous difference of scale—as of one single drop measured against the bitter and stormy immensity of an ocean...[3]

Despite the necessary modesty of these sentiments, these remarks make clear that in a fundamental way this novel is itself an act of solidarity, an attempt to make fiction adequate to the 'trials' of participating in the 'immensity' of fearful events which one is powerless to control. The assumptions of youth, 'care-free and fervent', yield, after such trials, to a maturer and stoical sense of one's own limitations, a form of self-possession whose acknowledgment of loss and suffering includes also an enhanced sense of one's real capabilities, and a pronounced need for kinds of fellow-feeling. These attitudes are more or less explicit in the 'Author's Note', as in the scene at the end of the tale when the narrator comes across Giles on his return to port:

> '... I'll tell you, Captain Giles, how I feel. I feel old. And I must be. All of you on shore look to me just a lot of skittish youngsters that have never known a care in the world.'
>
> He didn't smile. He looked insufferably exemplary. He declared:
>
> 'That will pass. But you do look older—it's a fact.'
>
> 'Aha!' I said.
>
> 'No, no! The truth is that one must not make too much of anything in life, good or bad.'

'Live at half-speed,' I murmured perversely. 'Not everyone can do that.'

'You'll be glad enough presently if you can keep going even at that rate,' he retorted, with his air of conscious virtue. 'And there's another thing: a man should stand up to his bad luck, to his mistakes, to his conscience and all that sort of thing. Why— what else would you have to fight against?'

I kept silent. I don't know what he saw in my face, but he asked abruptly:

'Why—you aren't faint-hearted?'

'God only knows, Captain Giles,' was my sincere answer.

'That's all right,' he said calmly. 'You will learn soon how not to be faint-hearted. A man has got to learn everything—and that's what so many of those youngsters don't understand.'

'Well, I am no longer a youngster.'

'No,' he conceded...[4]

The ironic touches by which the narrator presents Giles here, for all his wisdom, as a slightly complacent and moralizing figure suggest the presumption of being explicit or definitively authoritative or prescriptive about the attitude to life that his remarks nonetheless convey. It is an attitude which at this point the whole working of the tale conspires to vindicate:

> ...a man should stand up to his bad luck, to his mistakes, to his conscience and all that sort of thing... You will learn soon how not to be faint-hearted. A man has got to learn everything—and that's what so many of those youngsters don't understand...

This quotation works well as an introduction to the ethical attitude at the heart of *The Shadow-Line*. In *The Shadow-Line*, human dignity and any genuine degree of self-knowledge or autonomy depend in important ways, as Giles's words suggest, not on a prescribed morality of good and evil, a morality of 'conscience and all that sort of thing...', but on a belief that, in Giles's words, 'A man has got to learn everything' through responding without being 'faint-hearted' to the events which befall him, even as 'bad luck' or as a 'mistake'. The narrator expresses a similar attitude, rather reluctantly, at an early stage of his command:

> Yes. I had my hands full of complications which were most valuable as 'experience'. People have a great opinion of the advantages of experience. But in that connection experience means

always something disagreeable as opposed to the charm and
innocence of illusions.

I must say I was losing mine rapidly...[5]

More broadly, this chapter draws on Deleuze's work as a
way of conceptualizing in Conrad's text some of the issues that
have already been touched on: the belated status of consciousness vis-à-vis the outwardly bound encounters of the body and
soul, and the importance of sympathy as a way of describing
these as adventures of becoming whose import is ultimately
also political:

> Each individual is...himself composed of individuals of a lower
> order and enters into the composition of individuals of a higher
> order...[6]

Further, as has been suggested, through the author's remarks
above, or Giles's, the text is informed by a sense that such
sympathy is inseparable from a stoical acceptance of events in
which the phantasms of conscience must be resisted. Events
bring crises, 'complications', in which fortitude and imagination alone are productive ways of overcoming resentment and
remorse. In 'On the Superiority of Anglo-American Literature'
in *Dialogues*, Deleuze articulates a Spinozist ethic with a comple-
mentary emphasis on what can be termed a Stoic ethics of the
event:

> ...agents or patients, when we act or undergo, we must always
> be worthy of what happens to us. Stoic morality is undoubtedly
> this: not being inferior to the event, becoming the child of one's
> own events...[7]

To take one brief introductory example of how this text dramatizes these things: in the following critical moment in the
text, the narrator has to overcome his obscure and irrational
guilt over the loss of the quinine, and confess to the crew,
fearful as he is of their reproach:

> The words that passed between us were few and puerile in
> regard to the situation. I had to force myself to look them in the
> face. I expected to meet reproachful glances. There were none.
> The expression of suffering in their eyes was indeed hard
> enough to bear. But that they couldn't help. For the rest, I ask
> myself whether it was the temper of their souls or the sympathy

of their imagination that made them so wonderful, so worthy of
my undying regard.[8]

The provisional soundings of the final sentence, with its characteristic effect of circumspection—at once tentative and many-
sided—indicate an act of recapitulation which expresses formally a continuity with the open-ended nature of the event here,
as a moment in which the actualities of feeling surprise and stall
the operations of fearful prediction. Conrad's rhetoric here
typically uses its rhythmic cross-hatching phrases to make a
modest inconclusiveness a stimulus to further adventures of
thought:

> For the rest, I ask myself whether it was the temper of their souls
> or the sympathy of their imagination that made them so won-
> derful, so worthy of my undying regard...

In this way the act of writing recapitulates not only the earlier
events, but their status as 'marvels and mysteries', in that language as a form of expression becomes an adventure of participation, implicitly itself marvellous and mysterious, in which
the reader's creative powers and sympathies are elicited and
sustained. In the process, for an indefinite time also the reader's
individuality is enhanced by an incorporation into the larger
individuation which affects the group and narrator, and which
is effected for the reader by the singular workings of Conrad's
narrative.

In terms of writing, these emphases on the event and sympathy retain an essential relation to the productions of minor
literature, since they indicate how writing can draw the individual into what Deleuze terms new 'compounds or collectives,
assemblages':

> One must...write *with*. With the world, with a part of the world,
> with people...a conspiracy of love or hatred. There is no judge-
> ment in sympathy, but agreements of convenience between
> bodies of all kinds. This is assembling, being in the middle, on
> the line of encounter between an internal world and the external
> world...[9]

In this context, then, further, writing has the power to be an
event of becoming, of individuation as a function of association. It eludes the punctual logic of consciousness with its assumptions of the demarcated forms of object and subject.

Against this, fiction can take on an ethical and political power, as in this passage which ends with a reference to Crane's *The Red Badge of Courage* that is reminiscent of Conrad's novel:

> Verbs in the infinitive are limitless becomings. The verb to be has the characteristic—like an original taint—of referring to an I, at least to a possible one, which overcodes it and puts it in the first person of the indicative. But infinitive becomings have no subject: they refer only to an 'it' of the event (it is raining) and are themselves attributed to states of things which are compounds or collectives, assemblages... True novels operate with indefinites which are not indeterminate, infinitives which are not undifferentiated...'the young soldier' who leaps up and flees and sees himself leap up and flee, in Stephen Crane's book...[10]

'An Effect of that Force Somewhere'

The barest description of the events of Conrad's text makes clear the strange, unpredictable route of its narration—a young man inexplicably gives up his job; passes time rather pointlessly in a far Eastern seaport; then, with the good fortune to be offered a command, he embarks upon a seemingly ill-fated voyage in which communal effort appears to be the only means of surviving, and of overcoming, the forces ranged against his ship. At worst, these forces look as if they might be supernatural. At best they appear merely as forces of superstition and fear, interior phantasms unleashed by the chief officer, Burns, to prey upon the sailors. In any case, disaster threatens before the mysterious coming about of the ship's eventual delivery from danger.

Similarly, Conrad's writing in *The Shadow-Line* is, in its local texture, perpetually subject to enigmatic interruptions and indefinite movements that suspend the work of recognition or prediction. As an aspect of this, for the narrator the detail of the world impinges in perpetually surprising ways which can both confound and inspire. Similarly, Fredric Jameson has commented on how in Conrad's work the narrative subject is prey to kinds of intermittent discomposure and multiplication.[11] The individual senses and thought are surprised into intensified and separate moments of working by the obdurate materiality of things, or sounds, or the challenges which other people pose to the narrator's understanding. Although such encounters are problematic because they resist explanation, nonetheless their structure involves a kind of shock to the self in which also it is redeemed from false abstractions:

> Both binnacle lights went out. I suppose the water forced itself into them, though I wouldn't have thought that possible, for they fitted into the cowl perfectly...[12]

> The impetuosity of my advent made the man at the helm start slightly. A block aloft squeaked incomprehensibly, for what on earth could have made it do so. It was a whistling note like a bird's...[13]

Throughout the novel, there is a sense, as here, that real events and human actions provoke essentially multiple activities of thought and sense, resisting straightforward interpretation. Hence, the unnamed narrator meditates perpetually on the inadequacies, as well as the inescapability, of thinking of human behaviour in terms of the will and understanding. Customary narratives about life may insist on images of control, or command, but the unfolding of events, our participation in them, and what and how we may become is felt to be far more incalculable:

> This is not a marriage story. It wasn't so bad as that with me. My action, rash as it was, had more the character of divorce—almost of desertion. For no reason on which a sensible person could put a finger I threw up my job—chucked my berth—left the ship of which the worst that could be said was that she was a steamship and therefore, perhaps, not entitled to that blind loyalty which... However, it's no use trying to put a gloss on what even at the time I myself half suspected to be a caprice...[14]

The narrator's seemingly capricious impulse at leaving his steamship results in a period of boredom and uncertainty, before the lucky chance of his new command, and the return, for the time being, to a sense of purpose. These margins and intervals of the uncertain and enigmatic, then, unravel the purposiveness of narrator and character, and imbue the narrative with Conrad's inimitable sense of puzzling contingency—as when the ship is later seemingly fatefully becalmed, and then just as puzzlingly delivered. Perpetually also, in personal terms, the narrator remembers his own recurrent sense of self-estrangement at

moments that take on, however trivial they may seem, the aura
of a crisis or a test. Often he seems to be intently observing
himself, as if in a kind of waking dream. In such states direct
engagement with the novel's world seems suspended, even as
the prose takes on the most local sense of factual exactitude.
Details of sound and sight stand out with the puzzling immedi-
acy of things noticed in a dream or a fever:

> It's a good step from the Officers' home to the Harbour Office; but
> with the magic word 'Command' in my head I found myself
> suddenly on the quay as if transported there in the twinkling of
> an eye, before a portal of dressed white stone above a flight of
> shallow white steps.
>
> All this seemed to glide towards me swiftly. The whole great
> roadstead to the right was just a mere flicker of blue, and the dim
> cool hall swallowed me up out of the heat and glare of which I
> had not been aware till the very moment I passed in from it.
>
> The broad inner staircase insinuated itself under my feet
> somehow...[15]

The narrator constantly finds phrases which give the most
diminished sense of his volition, as in the verbs here ('I found
myself...as if transported... All this seemed to glide towards
me...the dim cool hall swallowed me up...The broad inner
staircase insinuated itself under my feet somehow...'). His
experience is diversified into small local sensations, things seen
or felt all the more intensely for the way they seem to act
upon him, to participate in, or even in some obscure way dictate, the shape which his experiences take. Accordingly, his
actions seem to the narrator, both in remembering and as
remembered, often the movements of someone spellbound,
someone who responds to strange hypnotic imperatives delivered by inanimate or inhuman things. Elsewhere, his actions
seem merely incalculable or impulsive, but similarly resistant to
understanding:

> To this day I don't know what made me call after him... Well, it
> was an impulse of some sort; an effect of that force somewhere
> within our lives which shapes them this way or that. For if these
> words had not escaped from my lips (my will had nothing to do
> with that) my existence would, to be sure, have been still a sea-
> man's existence, but directed on now to me utterly inconceivable
> lines.
>
> No. My will had nothing to do with it...[16]

And suddenly I left all this. I left it in that, to us, inconsequential manner in which a bird flies away from a comfortable branch. It was as though all unknowing I had heard a whisper or seen something. Well—perhaps![17]

I had never in my life felt more detached from all earthly goings on. Freed from the sea for a time, I preserved the sailor's consciousness of complete independence from all land affairs...[18]

I felt on my face the breath of unknown powers that shape our destinies...[19]

It was only another miraculous manifestation of that day of miracles. I parted from him as if he had been a mere symbol. I floated down the staircase. I floated out of the official and imposing portal. I went on floating along... And nothing in the way of abstraction could have equalled my deep detachment from the forms and colours of this world. It was, as it were, absolute...[20]

The sense of a self-division open to incalculable chances and becomings, the sense that we do things before we can understand or reflect on them, is not merely a feature of youthful impulse in this text, however, but an essential feature of the image of experience and its temporality that the text offers. Ultimately, as one obvious aspect of this, it implies that our relations to the contingencies of fact can only be a learning from experience. Like Captain Giles, in his empirical study of the archipelagos, preconceptions and predictions are unavailing where what is required is a combination of readiness, modesty, caution, opportunity and adventure. An acceptance of both the anxieties and opportunities of self-difference is the condition of an appropriate ethical openness. Further, Conrad's style gives an important sense of these issues. The ruminative elaborations and inconclusive recappings of the language, its probing encircling of its objects, indicates a sense both of the repeated necessity of interpretation, as well as of its belated nature and shortfall:

To this day I don't know what made me call after him...

In this empiricist world, inconclusiveness becomes not merely a kind of narrative principle, but also the measure of a scrupulous exactitude which does not try reductively to force meaning. Interpretation must ultimately be subject to suspension, as it is in a syntax which revisits repeatedly, but each time differently, the enigmatic material which it attempts to chart:

> Well, it was an impulse of some sort; an effect... No. My will had nothing to do with it...

The important feature here, for the purposes of the larger argument, is how, in this kind of narration, narrative consciousness is specified as a reactive mode, one which meditates in the in-between of events which it is ultimately powerless to control. When Deleuze says of Spinoza that for the latter, 'consciousness is...the awareness of the passage', an effect of transitions between bodily totalities of more or less potent kinds, this statement could extend also to Conrad also, for this reason among others.[21] It is interesting in this respect to reflect on how critics have often denigrated the initial part of the tale, which tells of the youthful narrator's prolonged, rather desultory, sojourn in Singapore, as a failure of narrative economy and tension. Yet *The Shadow-Line* is a narrative above all which configures the experience of consciousness in a time of drift in which it attempts to catch up with, or anticipate, events that are beyond its influence. Persistently, the narrative stages the narrative consciousness in these ways as occupied within a time between an uncertain passivity and surprising movement, as in the ultimate denouement of the sea voyage where days of calm yield, after Burns's laughter, to sudden unaccountable motion.

This crucial moment in the text is important also, of course, in the way in which Burns's laughter seems, like the Ancient Mariner's blessing of the seabirds, a moment in which human dignity emerges through an overcoming of the fixations of guilt and the presumptions of interiority. Though this is merely one possibility within the ultimately complex kinds of indeterminacy and tentativeness which give the tale its particular texture, it is nevertheless germane to this discussion's recurrent critical emphasis on the limits of such attitudes and fixations. As an obvious aspect of this, the narrator is never further from understanding things than at those moments when, during the first sections of the tale, he arrogantly assumes his right to a command over them, misconstruing, for instance, Giles's kindly and wise counsel as a sort of mental instability:

> It never occurred to me then that I didn't know in what sound-
> ness of mind exactly consisted, and what a delicate and upon the
> whole, unimportant matter it was...[22]

So, in the early part of the tale, Giles's reticence, attentiveness, and tact helps to steer, as it were, with the minimum of direct intervention, the narrator to his new command. In an opposing way, the interferences of the Chief Steward, as he tries to manipulate people and events, come to grief by virtue of his very presumption. Both characters remain in their ways enigmatic, yet in importantly different ways, and the narrator's holding off from definitiveness is in fact the condition of complex kinds of intervention and orientation on the reader's part, no less than is Giles's in relation to the youthful narrator. In both cases, consciousness recovers a kind of power and appropriateness where it becomes attentive, and refuses a direct and totalizing grasp. In the same way, the language of the text schools the reader in taking up a position where consciousness finds an interim validity and function, a saving provisionality and modesty. Consciousness exists on a kind of bridge to which information of all kinds is referred, but secondarily, out of the real and diverse encounters which influence movement.

However, there is more to the novel's treatment of consciousness than this endorsing of a kind of reduced status for it, before the precedence of the multiplicities in which the individual is always taken up. Deleuze's discussion of Spinoza's *Ethics* allows for a drawing out of several other important threads here also. Spinoza, it has been said, contests the pretensions of consciousness, seeing it as a secondary domain of reflection, wherein are reproduced the *ideas of the ideas of the mind* as representations involved with the plural sensitivities of the body as relational potentials. It follows from this, as Deleuze says, that

> we are only conscious of the ideas that express the effect of
> external bodies on our own, ideas of affections...[23]

There is implicit here a whole ethical, political and speculative narrative, definable as the parallel emancipation of desire and consciousness from their enthralment by the inadequate ideas which occur under the specific conditions of consciousness.

These ideas are inadequate, in Spinoza's terminology, because they are expressions of a passivity, 'traces of an external body on our body'.[24] And so, consciousness, as reflection, is 'completely immersed within the unconscious' of the mind and body. The crucial question that emerges here, however, is how can consciousness be raised to a new kind of power, while being delivered from its false pretensions to control, and its status as a register of the effects of other bodies? The crucial part of the answer, for Deleuze and Spinoza, is that consciousness must become a rational party to an investigation of the true causes of its own knowledge, and so party to an enhanced knowledge which investigates the body's capabilities through the formation of adequate ideas of the body's relations. The formation of these is commensurate with the production of active affects, and the critique of the intrinsic illusions of consciousness itself.

As discussed in Chapter 2 above, the common notion is the important term for this type of adequate idea, in which is represented

> the composition of real relations between existing modes or individuals…as they are necessarily embodied in living beings, with the variable and concrete terms between which they are established. In this sense, the common notions are more biological than mathematical, forming a natural geometry that allows us to comprehend the unity of composition of all of Nature and the modes of variation of that unity…[25]

What is at stake in this ethical process is also what could be termed a psychotherapeutic dimension, the means by which behaviour can be construed in its true habitual passivity, as in Spinoza's famous dictum as to the misguidedness of the alcoholic who believes he speaks freely when he says under the influence what he later regrets. Behaviour as unconsciously determined by a neurotic imagination is the habitual embodiment of the relations out of which consciousness is formed, even as these traces constrain it to sadness. The introductory remarks to this chapter suggested Burns as a character who shows these contagious and confining powers of resentment. Unable to shake off the imagined and enslaving sense of a past subjection, his relation with the dead captain, he is obsessed in ways which are potentially ruinous to all on board. In his imagination he is haunted by the sense that the dead captain will reduce all efforts to impotence and destruction. In the Author's Note, Conrad explicitly traces the origins of superstition to negative emotion:

> ...those vain imaginings common to all ages...that in themselves are enough to fill all lovers of mankind with unutterable sadness. As to the effect of a mental or moral shock on a common mind, it is quite a legitimate subject for study and description. Mr Burns's moral being receives a severe shock in his relations with his late captain, and this in his diseased state turns into a mere superstitious fancy compounded of fear and animosity...[26]

The whole tale can accordingly be seen as a dramatizing of the challenges and complexities of such shocks and states of mind, as I have suggested, and of the need to find ways of resisting the relapse into a merely troubled and defensive sense of self-dignity, and contaminating kinds of neurosis.

As a further example of these things, here is an extract from the narrator's earliest encounter with the Chief Steward:

> It was a strange room to find in the tropics. Twilight and stuffiness reigned in there. The fellow had hung enormously ample, dusty, cheap lace curtains over his windows, which were shut. Piles of cardboard boxes, such as milliners and dressmakers use in Europe, cumbered the corners; and by some means he had procured for himself the sort of furniture that might have come out of a respectable parlour in the East End of London—a horsehair sofa, arm-chairs of the same. I glimpsed grimy antimacassars scattered over that horrid upholstery, which was awe-inspiring, insomuch that one could not guess what mysterious accident, need, or fancy had collected it there. Its owner had taken off his tunic, and in white trousers and a thin, short-sleeved singlet prowled behind the chair-backs nursing his meagre elbows...[27]

The description of the Steward's 'den' intensifies, on one level, potentials of speculation as to his psychological fixations and dilemmas. In the reader's mind fascination opens momentarily like a fan. So, the room can appear to specify something of the man's defensive and equivocal exile from a domestic past. One could, perhaps, multiply examples from the passage and

elsewhere as to how the anxiety of this reclusive and paranoid
character appears as merely perpetuated through a regressive
involvement, even identification, with a femininity at once
mourned and, one suspects, feared:

> The papers were old and uninteresting, filled up mostly with
> dreary stereotyped descriptions of Queen Victoria's first jubilee
> celebrations...[28]

If such lines of reading are unavoidably suggested by the
narrative, however, their explanatory determinations are not
finally endorsed by it. Conrad's type of description is so
pleasurable because it draws out the reader's intelligence and
perception in this way. Contradictory kinds of attitude spin
round, more or less subliminally, like spokes on a wheel as we
encounter the Chief Steward—we feel solicitude and interest
on the one hand; a slightly more defensive and reticent disen-
gagement on the other. His room becomes a domain of signs
which activates the reader's mind in multiple and changing
ways, by virtue of the narrative's way of emphatically and
perpetually involving its description of facts with irreducible
levels of query, opacity, and surprise. Reading is occasioned
by the shocks and stimuli of encounters which, once again,
suspend any settling out at an interpretive terminus:

> It was a strange room to find in the tropics...and by some means
> he had procured for himself the sort of furniture...one could not
> guess what mysterious accident, need, or fancy had collected it
> there...

So then, such set-pieces are always bordered by a kind of
astonishment or suspension of finality, as at the end of the tale
when the question of the worthwhileness of the whole adventure hangs over the arrival at port, and the parting of the
narrator and Ransome. In the description of Bangkok, this takes
the form of a testing compound of excitement and dread:

> There it was, spread largely on both banks, the Oriental capital
> which had as yet suffered no white conqueror; an expanse of
> brown houses of bamboo, of mats, of leaves, of a vegetable-matter
> style of architecture, sprung out the brown soil on the banks of
> the muddy river. It was amazing to think that in those miles of
> human habitations there was not probably half a dozen pounds
> of nails. Some of those houses of sticks and grass, like the nests of

an aquatic race, clung to the low shores. Others seemed to grow out of the water; others again floated in long anchored rows in the very middle of the stream. Here and there in the distance, above the crowded mob of low, brown roof ridges, towered great piles of masonry, king's palace, temples, gorgeous and dilapidated, crumbling under the vertical sunlight, tremendous, overpowering, almost palpable, which seemed to enter one's breast with the breath of one's nostrils and soak into one's limbs through every pore of one's skin...[29]

Response, suspended here between openness and guardedness, is in many further ways shadowed by a sense of the possibilities for experience which are offered by this alienating and incomprehensible city. Unconquered, a place whose architecture partakes of the qualities of vegetation rather than of engineering as such, its mesmerizing power and effect is conveyed by a language which becomes subject to proliferating, paratactic series of words and phrases. This syntax seems powerless to dictate a form to the materials of language and experience, and these take on hypnotic rhythms of their own in the process. So, for instance, in the final sentence, the adjective 'tremendous' floats on the surface of the language, before its anchoring reference becomes clear. It refers to the 'sunlight' whose intensity is experienced as an absolute kind of physical fact, threatening in its palpability, but also invigorating through its strangeness and its challenge to thought:

> Here and there in the distance, above the crowded mob of low, brown roof ridges, towered great piles of masonry, king's palace, temples, gorgeous and dilapidated, crumbling under the vertical sunlight, tremendous, overpowering, almost palpable, which seemed to enter one's breast with the breath of one's nostrils and soak into one's limbs through every pore of one's skin...

'A Sense of the Intensity of Existence'

In *The Logic of Sense*, Deleuze meditates on the resources that Stoic philosophy offers for what could be called an ethics of the event:

> Either ethics makes no sense at all, or this is what it means and has nothing else to say: not to be unworthy of what happens to us...[30]

Unworthiness here bears on what Deleuze sees as the traps of resignation or *ressentiment* as responses to what occurs. Against this, the Stoic seeks to will and understand the ways in which physical states of affairs as the interaction of bodies, violent or harmonious, express metaphysical events which exceed the accidents of their physical actualization. The event differs in nature, since, firstly, it has the temporal form of a becoming which is expressed in the encounter of bodies, but as an 'incorporeal effect',[31] referring simultaneously to an unlimited past and future:

> There is a strict complementarity between the two: between physical things in the depths and metaphysical events on the surface... The event is always produced by bodies which collide, lacerate each other or interpenetrate, the flesh and the sword. But this effect itself is not of the order of bodies... If the infinitives 'to die', 'to love', 'to move', to smile', etc., are events, it is because there is a part of them which their accomplishment is not enough to realize, a becoming in itself which constantly both awaits us and precedes us, like a third person of the infinitive, a fourth person singular. Yes, dying is engendered in our bodies, comes about in our bodies, but it comes from the Outside, singularly incorporeal, falling upon us like the battle which skims over the combatants... Love is in the depth of bodies, but also on that incorporeal surface which engenders it...[32]

Deleuze describes events here in terms of infinitives, 'to love', 'to die', to suggest that these are real but virtual entities which insist or inhere in states of affairs, as potentials of individuation which are expressed in occurrences without being exhaustively identifiable with the states of bodies to which they are attributed. This is so since the logic of events is not that of an objective and strictly representable state of affairs, but of a becoming, and a virtual power of difference implicated, and actualized repetitiously, in things and expressed in words.[33] This distinction between a physical order of the present, and the metaphysical effects of becoming, divided between past and future, engenders for the Stoic, on Deleuze's reading, an ethics which attempts to participate in the event through affirmation:

> *Amor fati*, to want the event, has never been to resign oneself, still less to play the clown or the mountebank, but to extract from our actions and passions that surface refulgence, to *counter-effectuate*

the event, to accompany that effect without body, that part which goes beyond the accomplishment, the immaculate part... Between the cries of physical pain and the songs of metaphysical suffering, how is one to trace one's narrow, Stoical way, which consists in being worthy of what happens, a light, an encounter, an event, a speed, a becoming...extracting the pure event which unites me with those whom I love, who await me no more than I await them, since the event alone awaits us...[34]

The discussion above emphasized how the texture of Conrad's tale is imbued with a sense of the event, of encounters, as when the interpolated and indefinite recapitulations of the narrator divide the moment of narration itself, configuring it as a time of unknowing quest in which one's powers of comprehension are both challenged and exceeded. In the larger movement of the tale, such challenges and uncertainties involve real threats to the young captain's self-composure. The narrator's crossing of the shadow-line, from early unreflective and untested youth, involves an intensified awareness of the potentially annihilating and isolating nature of events, their unmeaning recalcitrance conveying an inescapable and irresolvable objectivity that forces thought and defies comprehension:

> The impenetrable blackness beset the ship so close that it seemed by thrusting one's hand over the side one could touch some unearthly substance. There was in it an effect of inconceivable terror and of inexpressible mystery...[35]

Accordingly, on his return to shore, after the experience of the 'deadly stillness' of the voyage,[36] the narrator is struck by an incongruous sense of 'the springy step, the lively eyes, the strong vitality of every one I met...'[37] Nonetheless, although the novel is imbued with a pronounced sense of accident, of all the confounding brutality and opacity of fact, it combines this with a conviction that the sensible world expresses 'marvels, mysteries', if the spirit can respond without resignation or disappointment. In such an attitude there is a sense of fate, of necessity, in that the actual is embraced as an opportunity for self-discovery:

> With every event, there is indeed the present moment of its actualization, the moment in which the event is embodied in a state of affairs, an individual, or a person, the moment we designate by saying, 'here, the moment has come'.[38]

The narrator's first hearing of his new command with his ship is presented as just such a moment, in which the chance of the waiting ship seems a summons to which he responds with 'a sense of the intensity of existence':

> A ship! My ship! She was mine, more absolutely mine for possession and care than anything in the world; an object of responsibility and devotion. She was there waiting for me, spellbound, unable to move, to live, to get out into the world (till I came), like an enchanted princess. Her call had come to me as if from the clouds. I had never suspected her existence. I didn't know how she looked, I had barely heard her name, and yet we were indissociably united for a certain portion of our future, to sink or swim together.
>
> A sudden passion of anxious impatience rushed through my veins and gave me such a sense of the intensity of existence as I have never felt before or since. I discovered how much a seaman I was, in heart, in mind, and, as it were, physically—a man exclusively of sea and ships; the sea the only world that counted, and the ships the test of manliness, of temperament, of courage and fidelity—and of love...[39]

6 |

Virginia Woolf—*The Voyage Out*

This chapter describes some of the uses Woolf makes of the idea of movement in this her earliest novel, bearing in mind Deleuze and Guattari's linking of Woolf's fiction with the concept of movement in *A Thousand Plateaus*, as well as some pertinent aspects of Deleuze's analyses of movement in *Bergsonism* and his books on cinema. Above all, the concentration in these following pages is on how Woolf's writing in *The Voyage Out* conveys to the reader the characters' participation in modes of relation, and in currents of feeling and perception, that carry them for an indefinite interval outside of their singular identities and their habitual and social ideas of self.

This is not to deny the readings of critics such as, respectively, Sue Roe and Clare Hanson, who have demonstrated the ways in which the love relationships in the novel, such as that between Rachel and Terence, or Susan and Arthur, can be said importantly to fail:

> Woolf drafted this difficult novel, ostensibly about the heroine's rite of passage into womanhood seven agonising times, and as many times attempted to solve the problem of sexual inertia. But the trouble was (as Woolf herself dimly perceived) that she needed to depict for Woolf a psychological transition which she was simply unable to imagine...[1]

> Rachel's illness and death are explicitly connected in the text with her repudiation of sexuality...[2]

In this aspect, the text can be seen as expressing a rejection of marriage and sexual consummation, such as seems apparent in Woolf's plan for an early dramatic collaboration with Jack Hills about

> a man and woman...never meeting...but all the time you'll feel
> them come nearer...—but when they almost meet—only a door
> between—you see how they miss...[3]

Nonetheless, it is possible to read such a remark as also compatible with the novel's fascination with movements and emotions which operate outside conscious intentions and the desti-
nations of conjugality and the sexual act ('but all the time you'll
feel them coming nearer'), and which express feeling within a
'bloc of becoming' in Deleuze's phrase. In 'A Sketch of the
Past', Woolf makes a statement in which images of music and
art convey a sense of how such participations themselves access
larger movements of immanence:

> From this I reach what I might call a philosophy; at any rate it is
> a constant idea of mine; that behind the cotton wool is hidden a
> pattern; that we—I mean all human beings are connected with
> this; that the whole world is a work of art; that we are parts of the
> work of art. In *Hamlet* or a Beethoven quartet is the truth about this
> vast mass that we call the world. But there is no Shakespeare,
> there is no Beethoven; certainly and emphatically there is no
> God; we are the words; we are the music; we are the thing
> itself...[4]

The text uses many means to dramatize repeatedly for the characters the kinds of self-dissociation and self-alteration involved
in the relation by movement of closed repetitive possibilities of
identity to new ensembles which express different, fluctuating,
transformational potentials of the terms involved. Part of the
argument of this chapter, further, will be concerned with relating these aspects of the text to its modes of expression, and its
singular kinds of affective working on the reader. Most obviously, as this probably suggests, the discussion aligns pertinent
aspects of the Bergsonian distinction of space and time with
Woolf's recurrent exploration in her novel of what can be
simply termed the distinction of the closed and the open. That
is, an exploration of a kind of inescapable counterpointing in
experience as, in an important aspect, between the requirements and necessities of social identity, and the equally inevitable, deterritorialized, externally related constructions of
desire. There are many aspects to this exploration of becoming
in Woolf, and this entrance into movement is conveyed in the

text as both joyful and perilous. It is both the fullest expression of the spirit through sensation, emotion and artistic endeavour, and also unsustainable, even fated to dissociation and loss.

Before developing the terms of this chapter's alignment of Woolf's work with Bergson, however, it is important to multiply some cautionary remarks. Woolf, it seems, had not read Bergson by 1922, nor even her sister-in-law's book on him, *Misuse of the Mind,* as Harvena Richter notes in a footnote:

> According to a letter written by Leonard Woolf to James Hanley, Virginia had not read Bergson or even Karin Stephen's book on him in 1922...[5]

Nevertheless, Richter makes some pertinent points about the consonance of Woolf's literary work with Bergson's philosophical venture, beginning with the way Woolf's moments of being involve an intensive sense of time. This makes an indivisible unity of heterogeneous and multiple states and levels of consciousness and emotion, as the spirit expresses itself in the body's compounding with the elements of the outside. Accordingly, the moment of a summer night becomes a haecceity, in which the operations of personality and the clock are displaced by the emergence of a different symbiotic assemblage:

> By the clock, the span of the moment of being might be merely five minutes or five seconds. Experienced emotionally/mentally, it is seen to be composed, as is her moment of a summer's night, of a multiplicity of states of consciousness, a succession of awarenesses which take place not in five minutes—which posits a past, present and future—but the all-inclusive *now.* Although Mrs Woolf did not consciously follow Bergson, her moment of being, with its diversity in unity resembles his concept of duration in which time is qualitative, nonspatial, real, vertical, and always present.[6]

As Richter makes clear, it is not a question of reducing Woolf's literary practice to Bergson's philosophical writings, or of arguing for any direct contact between their work, but of asking what a reading of Woolf can gain conceptually from being read alongside a body of work whose concerns are powerfully sympathetic to those of Woolf. Richter continues with some remarks which link these points about psychic duration to Bergson's meditations in *Creative Evolution* on how for every living thing 'the body is changing form at every moment', so that 'what is real is the continual *change* of form: *form is only a snapshot view of a transition*'.[7]

> Thus real (or psychological) time for the character may pass quickly or slowly, in response to emotional states such as excitement or boredom. It can contract or expand, contracting to attention of a single present fact or state, or expanding to include simultaneous memories from one or more periods of past time... The way the character experiences time, therefore, is another method of imparting to the reader the particular quality of that character's state of consciousness. We might term this, for lack of a definition, *rate of experience*, or rate of being. Being is always moving, never static. Indeed, as Bergson explains, time or duration is actually the psychical state of becoming, poised on the brink between past and future and exhibiting qualities of motion, growth and change comparable to the biological processes in which every tissue and fluid of the body are in a state of constant transformation. In that sense, man does not experience time as such, but rather sensation, motion, change. Experiencing the wealth of the myriad impressions of one moment of consciousness, he is in transition to a new moment which the duration he has just passed through will enrich...[8]

Clear and cogent as Richter's remarks are, it is necessary before going on to discuss *The Voyage Out* to develop further some of the philosophical staging for the discussion of the novel. In the first chapter of *Cinema I*, Deleuze offers an analysis of Bergson's account of movement in *Creative Evolution* in terms of a metaphysics of becoming. Deleuze begins with the famous distinction between movement as a concrete, indivisible, and imperceptible activity of covering, and space as the instantaneously given and quantitatively divisible field covered. For Deleuze, this difference requires itself to be thought appropriately in terms of time, duration. Such a thinking goes against metaphysical imperatives that would seek to assimilate movement to space, and in which time would be conceived according to the logic of positions and abstract points. So here movement needs to be thought as involving not merely the transposition of material bodies, but also as expressing their changes. Bodies in movement (and through movement) participate in qualitative alterations. Deleuze gives as an example of this Bergson's example from *Creative Evolution* where one waits for sugar to dissolve in a glass of water:

> But what is his main point? That the movement of translation which detaches the sugar particles and suspends them in the water itself expresses a change in the whole, that is in the content of the glass; a qualitative transition from water which contains a sugar lump to the state of sugared water. If I stir with the spoon, I speed up the movement, but I also change the whole, which now encompasses the spoon, and the accelerated movement continues to express the change of the whole. 'The wholly superficial displacements of masses and molecules studied in physics and chemistry would become, by relation to that inner vital movement (which is transformation and not translation) what the position of moving object is to the movement of that object in space...'[9]

The identification of the inner nature of movement with vitality is an important one here, and it leads into the main metaphysical point. Movement is not simply a function by which a body changes its position in space, but a function of ontological relatedness in which the body's qualities change as a function of their association within a larger and open and changing whole, defined in terms of duration:

> movement relates the objects of a closed system to open duration, and duration to the object of the system which it forces to open up. Movement relates the objects between which it is established to the changing whole which it expresses, and vice versa. Through movement the whole is divided up into objects, and objects are re-united in the whole, and indeed between the two 'the whole' changes...[10]

In the discussion of movement which takes in Woolf in *A Thousand Plateaus*, Deleuze and Guattari write of movement in terms of the relative planes of transcendence and immanence, in ways which indicate an important Bergsonian inspiration, while also recasting it in the characteristically rhizomatic means of argumentation of that text. However, it is an important and relevant discussion not only because it relates Woolf's art to the idea of movement, but because it articulates the concept of movement with questions of art, subjectivity and society more explicitly than in the above discussion in *Cinema I*, and, further, in ways which link with Woolf's own statement above from 'A Sketch of the Past'. Above all, Deleuze and Guattari emphasize the powers of movement to elude the formal presuppositions of perception and recognition as momentary acts of a subject operating according to the representative values of 'the plane of organization and development'.[11] As has been noted in Chapter 1 above, however, such a plane of formed objects and subjects, and defined chronological moments, remains in reciprocal presupposition with the related 'plane of immanence or consistency', from which such forms emerge, and to which movement pertains.[12] On this latter plane, the demarcations of organic bodies, and of punctual temporal instants, are disarticulated in the indefinite duration of becomings, haecceities, or individuations, as functions of the adventitious combinings of bodies. To cite this discussion is also to indicate further how Bergson becomes a particularly relevant figure for a discussion of Woolf. Beyond the vocabulary of duration and movement, for instance, one can discern in the discussion in *A Thousand Plateaus* other notions relevant to *The Voyage Out*, as when Deleuze and Guattari connect the concept of movement with notions of creativity and emotion that relate to Bergson's intermittent discussions of art and mysticism in *The Two Sources of Morality and Religion*.[13]

To make this point, a quotation of Deleuze's discussion of Bergson's identification of artistic and mystical activity in *Bergsonism* precedes a comparable extract from the discussion which introduces Woolf in *A Thousand Plateaus*:

> Thus the great souls—to a greater extent than philosophers—are those of artists and mystics... At the limit is the mystic who plays with the whole of creation, who invents an expression of it whose adequacy increases with its dynamism...[14]

> For everybody/everything is the molar aggregate, but *becoming everybody/everything* is another affair, one that brings into play the cosmos with its molecular components. Becoming everybody/everything (*tout le monde*) is to world (*faire monde*), to make a world (*faire un monde*)...[Virginia Woolf] says that it is necessary to 'saturate every atom', and to do that it is necessary to eliminate all that is resemblance and analogy, but also 'to put everything into it': eliminate everything that exceeds the moment, but put in everything that it includes—and the moment is not the instantaneous, it is the haecceity into which

one slips and that slips into other haecceities by transparency...
one has made a necessarily communicating world... One has
combined 'everything' (*le 'tout'*): the indefinite article, the in-
finitive-becoming, and the proper name to which one is
reduced...[15]

The creative desire described in the second passage here, working in the production of immanent associations between molecular elements, can be construed in terms of movement, as of a
wave that takes up the motions of smaller elements into a larger
individuation, and which establishes co-resonating and co-functioning relations between them, altering each outside of their
pre-given form or organization. Further, such a desire also participates in the repetition of virtual or ideal potentials, actualized in ever variable and different forms. In this way, desire
enters into the repetition of a becoming that in Deleuze and
Guattari's terms is party to the becoming of a world. For
Bergson, this link between the world and the differentiations of
living beings is the movement of life and the life of movement,
as Deleuze puts it:

> The finality of the living being exists only insofar as it is essen-
> tially open onto a totality that is itself open: 'finality is external,
> or it is nothing at all'...it is not the whole that closes like an
> organism, it is the organism that opens onto a whole, like this
> virtual whole...[16]

'Her Mind Seemed to Enter into Communion'

The basic opposition between the open and the closed, then,
can be identified with the Bergsonian imperative to think of
things in terms of the creative self-variation which they produce
in duration, and not in terms of the static and perceivable
realities which can be discerned when we contemplate them in
terms of their spatial positions and chronological moments. In
this first part of the chapter, the aim is to look at how such a
distinction can be put to work with a description of the narrative values of Woolf's text. So, in *The Voyage Out*, the reader
repeatedly comes across scenes where difficulties of human
relatedness are expressed in spatial terms. In Chapter 1, there
are the uncommunicating solitudes of the Ambroses:

> He came up to her, laid his hand on her shoulder, and said,
> 'Dearest'. His voice was supplicating. But she shut her face away
> from him, as much as to say, 'You can't possibly understand...'[17]

The image of shutting away here is a prevalent one in the
novel, where the recoil into a pained sense of the difficulty of
making oneself understood goes along with the other person's
difficulty of understanding and responding. Nonetheless, the
narrative becomes itself a vehicle that traverses these distances
to varying degrees, by using its own language to convey movements of intimacy which function outside of the characters'
own speech and their defensive consciousnesses of self. Again,
an obvious case of this occurs towards the beginning of the
novel, where Helen watches Rachel asleep:

> Ten minutes later Mrs Ambrose opened the door and looked at
> her. It did not surprise her to find that this was the way in which
> Rachel passed her mornings. She glanced round the room at the
> piano, at the books, at the general mess. In the first place she
> considered Rachel aesthetically; lying unprotected she looked
> somehow like a victim dropped from the claws of a bird of prey,
> but considered as a woman of twenty-four, the sight gave rise to
> reflections, Mrs Ambrose stood thinking for at least two minutes.
> She then smiled, turned noiselessly away and went, lest the
> sleeper should waken, and there should be awkwardness of
> speech between them...[18]

The contents of Mrs Ambrose's reflections are unworded, inti-
mated by the narrator rather than made explicit. However, the
effect of the passage is nonetheless here to draw the reader into
the older woman's kind of privileged access into Rachel's singularity. It is an access of a complex or compound sort—Rachel's
unguarded attitude elicits various responses. Amusement at her
touching individuality mingles together with a more reflective
sense also of a certain typicality ('a woman of twenty-four...').
The reader participates in this intimate and unsocialized relay
of responses, before Mrs Ambrose 'turned noiselessly away...
lest the sleeper should awaken...'

There are many such scenes in the novel, where Woolf structures dramatic and affective moments around a condition of
solitude which appears compounded by society and language,
yet which can be displaced in its turn by the indefinite duration
of other kinds of rapport with which Woolf's modes of narra-

tion preserve their own inwardness. Mrs Dalloway's question, 'yet, how communicate' reverberates throughout the novel,[19] and is typical of the character's enhanced sense of what Hirst calls the 'circles' which people inhabit as social beings, or, to take Richard's image

> What solitary icebergs we are, Miss Vinrace! How little we can communicate... This reticence—this isolation—that's what's the matter with modern life...[20]

For Rachel, music is a means of inducing an absent-mindedness in which this isolation can be for an interval forgotten and overcome:

> Her efforts to come to an understanding had only hurt her aunt's feelings, and the conclusion must be that is better not to try. To feel anything strongly was to create an abyss between oneself and others who feel strongly perhaps but differently. It was far better to play the piano and forget all the rest... It appeared that nobody ever said a thing they meant... Absorbed by her music... Inextricably mixed in dreamy confusion, her mind seemed to enter into communion, to be delightfully expanded with the spirit of the whitish boards on deck, with the spirit of the sea, with the spirit of Beethoven, Op. 112...[21]

Such effects of expansion, paradoxical to common sense in their evocation of the 'confusion' or 'communion' of spiritual potentials outside of personality, are a means at once of participation, through affects, in other modes of being, as well as expressions of individuality. Once again, the narrative voice merges impersonally with Rachel's sense of things, to secure for it an enhanced mode of expression by which the reader is also drawn within Rachel's spiritual life. This is a solitude oblivious in its workings in this passage to the purely extensive divisions of the moment and of space, and to the failure of Rachel's attempted communication with her aunt. Accordingly, the syntactical closure of the sentence is counterpointed by a rhythm which corresponds to a drawing together of divergent elements into an inclusive arrangement. For Rachel, this is a creative 'individuation', as discussed in Chapter 1 above, where an altered quality of individuality emerges from encounters of all sorts:

> to be delightfully expanded with the spirit of the whitish boards

on deck, with the spirit of the sea, with the spirit of Beethoven, Op. 112...

As against these expansive and individuating effects of movement, the narrative constantly specifies, then, apparently intractable conditions of solipsistic separation. Throughout the novel, Woolf's narrator describes this in terms of images of spatial divisions, as of the walls that separate Hewet and Hirst, Miss Allan and Miss Warrington, Mr Ambrose and the rest of the party:

> Hewet retreated, pressing the poems of Thomas Hardy beneath his arm, and in their beds next door to each other the young men were soon asleep...[22]

> Very different was the room through the wall... As Miss Allan read her book, Susan Warrington was brushing her hair...[23]

> ...one room...possessed a character of its own because the door was always shut, and no sound of music or laughter issued from it. Everyone in the house was vaguely conscious that something went on behind that door, and without in the least knowing what it was, was influenced in their own thoughts by the knowledge that if they passed it the door would shut, and if they made a noise Mr Ambrose inside would be disturbed...[24]

These divisions of rooms, it is true, ensure a necessary privacy, as with Mrs Ambrose's promise to Rachel that she be allowed a room:

> Among the promises which Mrs Ambrose had made her niece should she stay was a room cut off from the rest of the house, large, private—a room in which she could play, read, think, defy the world, a fortress as well as a sanctuary. Rooms, she knew, became more like worlds than rooms at the age of twenty-four...[25]

Nonetheless, Woolf's novel is fundamentally concerned, as has been implied, with exploring and exemplifying imagined ways in which this sense of contraction and remoteness can be overcome by spiritual resources that are surprising or strange to conscious thought, and which, in the latter case, makes of Rachel's room a kind of world. In terms of human relations, the novel probes, and sets up in its own narrative forms of expression— what could be called suprapersonal kinds of contact. Human feeling and sympathy operate in indeterminate ways, where contact is felt rather than recognized, and which the narrative can only describe in terms of paradoxes. In the following case, for example, Clarissa Dalloway wakes to an amused idea of the others on board ship as having infiltrated her dreams. The strange suggestion of a collective unconscious here then passes into the narrative, where it is expanded to fully blown form, as the narrative describes the dreams that 'went from one brain to another':

> She then fell into a sleep, which was as usual extremely sound and refreshing, but visited by fantastic dreams of great Greek letters stalking around the room, when she woke up and laughed to herself, remembering where she was and that the Greek letters were real people, lying asleep not many yards away. Then, thinking of the black sea outside tossing beneath the moon, she shuddered, and thought of her husband and the others as companions on the voyage. The dreams were not confined to her indeed, but went from one brain to another. They all dreamt of each other that night, as was natural, considering how thin the partitions between them, and how strangely they had been lifted off the earth to sit next each other in mid-ocean, and see every detail of each other's faces, and hear whatever they chanced to say...[26]

The narrative voice in this passage, then, appears to operate in a region of non-conscious or superconscious existence. It moves out beyond the limits of an identifiable narrative persona, as the narrator enters into the larger movement of dreams which she describes, a movement which transcends the individuals who are subject to it, 'how strangely they had been lifted off the earth to sit next each other in mid-ocean...' Such movements, and the powers of sympathy and reflection which they require in being translated into art, can illuminatingly be juxtaposed, in finishing this section, with remarks by Bergson in *Creative Evolution*. Here, Bergson distinguishes the function of art from static visual representations such as are given to the eye. Art necessarily involves duration as the indivisible time of a sympathetic intuition which reflects on time as the opening of beings to movement and relation:

> Our eye perceives the features of the living being merely as assembled, not as mutually organized. The intention of life, the

simple movement that runs through the lines, that binds them
together and gives them significance, escapes it. This intention
is just what the artist tries to regain, in placing himself back
within the object by a kind of sympathy, in breaking down, by
an effort of intuition, the barrier that space puts up between him
and his model... Then, by the sympathetic communication
which it establishes between us and the rest of the living, by the
expansion of our consciousness which it brings about, it [intu-
ition] introduces us into life's own domain, which is reciprocal
interpenetration, endlessly continued creation...[27]

'A General Desire for Movement'

These emphases on movements are marked also in the text's
extraordinary representation of human emotion. For Woolf,
emotion is not ultimately identifiable with circumstantial, personal and social representations and determinations. In short,
Woolf's novel is concerned with countering the image of human
communication and the separations of identity which such an
objective scheme suggests, and with conveying a sense that the
potentials of human interrelation need to be thought and experienced differently. Here Mrs Dalloway's question, as to how
to communicate, can be thought about in relation to Deleuze
and Guattari's identification above of Woolf's art with the
creation of 'a necessarily communicating world', through its
dedication to the inclusive events of becoming which animate
the literary work. Before moving into further analysis of the
text, I want to draw some of these threads together further by
citing a passage from Deleuze's discussion of Bergson's account
of emotion. Although this passage is somewhat lengthy it articulates the interconnections of many of this chapter's preoccupations. Deleuze is writing about how Bergson conceptualizes
emotion as above all a potential of becoming, in distinction to
an account which links emotion to the recognizable representations which would explain it in terms of egoism and social
norms:

> But in both these cases, emotion is always connected to a repre-
> sentation on which it is supposed to depend. We are then placed
> in a composite of emotion and representation, without noticing
> that it is potential (*en puissance*), the nature of emotion as pure
> element. The latter in fact precedes all representation, itself

generating new ideas. It does not have, strictly speaking, an object, but merely an *essence* that spreads itself over various objects, animals, plants and the whole of nature. 'Imagine a piece of music which expresses love. It is not love for a particular person...the quality of love will depend upon its essence and not upon its object.' Although personal, it is not individual; transcendent, it is like the God in us. 'When music cries, it is humanity, it is the whole of nature which cries with it. Truly speaking, it does not introduce these feelings in us; it introduces us rather into them, like the passers-by that might be nudged in a dance.' In short, emotion is creative (first, because it expresses the whole of creation, then because *it* creates the work in which it is expressed; and finally, because it communicates a little of this creativity to spectators or hearers...)[28]

In this quotation emotion emerges as a generative power of difference, in which personal identity can be defined as a real but transitional effect, a moment of closure, an effect relative and subsequent, that is, to a creative movement which comes before it as an event, and which exceeds its logic. Further, Deleuze's discussion suggests the Bergsonian distinction between the relative dimensions of story-telling and creative emotional expression in literary art in *The Two Sources of Morality and Religion*, a distinction which has obvious pertinence to Woolf's aesthetic meditations on the potential 'life' of a literary work in an essay like *Modern Fiction*.[29]

To return to *The Voyage Out*, this chapter has begun an analysis of how the text expresses movements and events which draw the individuals concerned into affective groupings which tap more creative kinds of relation. An example of these things can be seen in the passages after Susan and Arthur's engagement has become a definite fact. Here, the narrator describes the enhanced physical sense that they have of each other. A kind of symbiosis has taken place between them, testifying to the affective powers of the body and spirit. Although this symbiosis impinges on their consciousnesses, it finds its articulation ultimately in the language of the narrative. Riding down the hill, in the passage quoted below, silence and distance are in reality cancelled by the common movement in which the characters are both involved, and for which riding provides a kind of metaphor. The larger movement of emotion is represented as drawing Susan and Arthur out of their purely subjective interiority, and personal history, involving them within an openended movement of indefinite duration, a movement out in which they are both altered. Once again, Woolf's unfolding of this, her attunement to these larger movements, is inseparable from her intense sense of the event, the singularity of the conjunction of Arthur and Susan, as well as from her sense that it occupies a temporality at odds with the chronology of purely sequential moments. In such passages in the novel, this kind of narrative engagement emerges as an extreme attentiveness, as if the narrative voice has become a vehicle by which Woolf's creative powers and individuality can be most fully expressed, through a kind of awareness in which any other kind of consciousness is for a moment set aside. There is an absolute intentness and sensitivity in the writing which appears adjusted to catch all the vibrations that play between the characters:

> The rush and embrace of the rockets as they soared up into the air seemed like the fiery way in which lovers suddenly rose and united, leaving the crowd gazing up at them with strained white faces. But Susan and Arthur, riding down the hill, never said a word to each other, and kept accurately apart.
>
> Then the fireworks became erratic, and soon they ceased altogether, and the rest of the journey was made almost in darkness, the mountain being a great shadow behind them, and bushes and trees little shadows which threw darkness across the road. Among the plane trees they separated, bundling into carriages and driving off, without saying good-night, or saying it only in a half-muffled way.
>
> It was so late that there was no time for normal conversation between their arrival at the hotel and their retirement to bed...[30]

And so the chapter moves to an end, with Susan lying in bed:

> She lay for a considerable time looking blankly at the wall opposite, her hands clasped above her, and her light burning by her side. All articulate thought had long ago deserted her; her heart seemed to have grown to the size of a sun, and to illuminate her entire body, shedding like the sun a steady tide of warmth...[31]

Of course, this power of emotion and mutual openness is subject to circumstances in the text, and Susan and Arthur part, and lapse back into their slightly doltish social personas. Nevertheless, the transports are presented as real, as real or more real than anything else, yet unsustainable. Woolf conveys marvellously the unspoken communion between the characters:

> But Susan and Arthur, riding down the hill, never said a word to
> each other, and kept accurately apart...

The simple adverb 'accurately' here has an effect of expansiveness, conveying their enhanced physical sense of each other, and the social and physical orders of things with which their 'keeping apart' outwardly conforms. The word is inward with this alteration in their relation, then, but it also conveys a sense of joy not only common but private, and expressed by Susan when she returns to her bedroom. Palpable as the reality of emotion is at this moment for the characters, narrator and reader, it is mysterious, inexplicable, paradoxical to describe. Paradoxical, because it is both something that carries the characters along outside themselves, as well as something which each carries within him or herself, as the fullest expression of their being; and also because the text represents it as something that seems at once to transcend the closures of time, and to be also purely transient in chronological terms. It appears as unaccountable in its defiance of logic as the movements of the rockets in their defiance of gravity, and their power to transform themselves utterly in an instant before their descent to earth and their reduction to ash. In this passage, as throughout the novel, fireworks take on a profound figural importance to express movements, alterations, momentary annihilations of distance and darkness, joyous illuminations linked in the passage to the powers of love, but qualified also as inevitably prey to extinction. The fireworks express as well an inspiration of art, towards unity and intensity, after which the earth-bound figures can only strain:

> The rush and embrace of the rockets as they soared up into the
> air seemed like the fiery way in which lovers suddenly rose
> and united, leaving the crowd gazing up at them with strained
> white faces...

More broadly, within this episode what is moving for the reader (amusing also to an important degree) in this description of the couple is a sense of their readiness at this moment for the future. Throughout the novel, Woolf's narrative values are inseparable from an affirmation of a preparedness, however tentatively, to move outside of what you have been, to remain true to the potential intensities or adventures which define life. This is despite all the pathos which attaches to the counter sense of these movements as fated in the social and circumstantial scheme of things. Hewet voices this in his comment to Evelyn, again through an image of fire:

> 'We don't care for people because of their qualities,' he tried to explain. 'It's just them that we care for,'—he struck a match— 'just that,' he said, pointing to the flames...[32]

In this novel, as in the others discussed in this book, moral qualities as such can be distinguished from the ethical values which inform the text. *The Voyage Out* is animated by such an insistence on the value of life as lying in intermittent events of conjunction. In such events the sympathies and affections are extended, through more indeterminate effects of movement or resonance. There is an interval in which the spirit is expressed through its encounters, and in which the material is raised to the power of the ideal, the temporal to the eternal. Rachel's piano playing is one kind of further image of this, as in the passage quoted above, as is the group which Hewet sets dancing. Another example is when Helen's dancing draws the two ladies looking on into an involuntary but common physical response:

> Her beauty, now that she was flushed and animated, was more expansive than usual, and both the ladies felt the same desire to touch her.
>   'I *am* enjoying myself,' she panted. 'Movement—isn't it amazing?'[33]

The word 'involuntary' is important, because the responsiveness which the narrative concentrates on in such moments is an expression of a creative autonomy that is rediscovered through physical relations. Paradoxically, perhaps, to a thinking which equates freedom with conscious operations of choice, the involuntariness of the response is an index here of a truer expressive autonomy than that of will. In a similar way, when Terence and Rachel talk of love, they communicate a sense that it is something in which their participation is mysterious. Although their acquiescence and agency are undoubted, they are also each fully aware that their common feeling is unaccountable, precarious, and that they can relapse moment by moment into estrangement:

> ...they remained uncomfortably apart; drawn so close together, as she spoke, that there seemed no division between them, and the next moment separate and far away again. Feeling this painfully, she exclaimed, 'It will be a fight...'[34]

> It was long before they moved, and when they moved it was with great reluctance. They stood together in front of the looking-glass, and with a brush tried to make themselves look as if they had been feeling nothing all morning, neither pain nor happiness. But it chilled them to see themselves in the glass, for instead of being vast and indivisible, they were really very small and separate, the size of the glass leaving a large space for the reflection of other things...[35]

The vocabulary here of an experience of vastness and indivisibility, associated with love, a sense that vanishes in the reflection, neatly summarizes the discussion here. Incalculable and unpredictable, its nature is to surprise, with common movements of feeling that are also once again feelings for movement:

> But the breeze freshened, and there was a general desire for movement... Occasional starts of exquisite joy ran through them, and then they were peaceful again...[36]

This last extract comes just after Terence and Rachel's avowal of their feeling for each other, during the journey down the river which will also bring about Rachel's death. This entwining of the enhancement of self with loss, of an effect of expansion with one of diminishment, is, it has been suggested, evident at all levels of the text's representation of human relations. Indeed it is evident in the disturbing image of perilous sensitivity which is applied to the first female in the whole of Woolf's fiction, Mrs Ambrose, who is said in Chapter 1 of the novel to have a mind 'like a wound exposed to dry in the air...'[37]

Again, one could locate this ambivalence, and the ethical aspect of a vulnerable openness, in the description of the ship in Chapter 2:

> ...an immense dignity had descended upon her; she was an
> inhabitant of the great world, which had so few inhabitants,
> travelling all day across an empty universe, with veils drawn
> before her and behind. She was more lonely than the caravan
> crossing the desert; she was infinitely more mysterious, moving
> by her own power and sustained by her own resources. The sea
> might give her death or some unexampled joy, and none would
> know of it. She was a bride going forth to her husband, a virgin
> unknown of men; in her vigour and purity she might be
> likened to all beautiful things, for as a ship she had a life of her
> own...[38]

The dignity attributed to the ship derives precisely from the
solitude and mystery which the narrator sees as intrinsic to its
progress. Sustained merely by its own power and resources the
ship moves between the past and an uncertain future, between
the 'veils drawn before her and behind', as the narrator puts it.
The ship remains poised between different possibilities, of
which the only certainty is that they will be different from
what has been. These are, as the narrator says, possibilities of
'death or unexampled joy', the phrase seeming, like much in
the passage, to anticipate Rachel's situation and fate. Moreover,
again the ship's loneliness in these respects is combined with a
sense of the beauty and possibilities of life and love: 'she was a
bride going forth to her husband, a virgin unknown of men; in
her vigour and purity she might be likened to all beautiful
things, for as a ship she had a life of her own...' As this implies,
however, it is as unstable anticipations that such expressive
movements have a real value in this text. Rachel's relation with
Terence, for whatever reasons, cannot arrive at social or sexual
consummation.[39] Interesting here, as always, is Woolf's description and prose style, which diversifies a description of the ship
into a series of images and metaphors which convey the unspoken emotion which it stimulates in the narrator. To put it
slightly differently, it is a series which actualizes the penumbra
of virtual emotion which surrounded her initial impression of
the ship, and which unfolds rhythmically and unguardedly in
ways which preserve in the relation of the narrator to ship a
purity of encounter such as is predicated of the ship itself in its
motion forwards.

'Her Dissolution Became so Complete...'

In this final part of the chapter I want to offer a more sustained account of how Woolf's narrative enters into the divisions within Rachel's own experience. Above all, the narrator is concerned with the ratio between the outwardly oriented movements of mind and body which are induced by perception, and the habitual sense of self and the recognizable world which returns to punctuate these. In Chapter 10, the narrator describes Rachel sitting in a chair, overcome by the oddness and singularity of the sounds from the garden, and by the 'exercise of reading' which 'left her mind contracting and expanding like the mainspring of a clock...' In line with this discussion she goes on to wonder:

> The sounds in the garden outside joined with the clock, and the small noises of midday, which one can ascribe to no definite cause, in a regular rhythm. It was all very real, very big, very impersonal, and after a moment or two she began to raise her first finger and to let it fall on the arm of her chair so as to bring back to herself some consciousness of her own existence... And life, what was that? It was only a light passing over the surface and vanishing, as in time she would vanish, though the furniture in the room would remain. Her dissolution became so complete that she could not raise her finger any more... It became stranger and stranger. She was overcome with awe that things should exist at all... She forgot that she had any fingers to raise... The things that existed were so immense and so desolate... She continued to be conscious of these vast masses of substance for a long stretch of time, the clock still ticking in the midst of the universal silence...[40]

Rachel's experience of dissolution is represented here as an ambivalent kind of yielding, in which she becomes open to the strange unity of the diverse elements of the surrounding scene at the same time as she surrenders an integrated sense of herself. As her attention mingles variously with the sounds from the garden, the unidentifiable and characteristic sounds of midday, the ticking of the clock, and so on, so these sounds induce a kind of entrancement in which the centripetal workings of self-consciousness and the organic workings of the body are for a time suspended. Her awareness of the scene is, accordingly,

both enhanced and diversified, and Woolf's narrative too, as
has been suggested before, here has a wonderful power to
evoke such familiar, subliminal activity. Further, the unconscious merging of Rachel's hearing with the aspects of the surrounding world develops into intimations that these multiple
elements of the scene form a whole or totality, though of a
kind that is open and fluctuating, and which, however marvellous, is also inhuman:

> It was all very real, very big, very impersonal, and after a
> moment or two she began to raise her first finger and to let it fall
> on the arm of her chair so as to bring back to herself some
> consciousness of her own existence... And life, what was that? It
> was only a light passing over the surface and vanishing, as in
> time she would vanish... She was overcome with awe that
> things should exist at all...The things that existed were so
> immense and so desolate...

It is difficult to do justice to the multiple and subtle ways in
which Woolf's writing is working here, as it conveys to the
reader the texture of Rachel's experience—the different moments of her outwardly bound perceptions, and their complex
syncopation with moments of reflection. The identification of
life and feeling throughout this text with the figure of movement is granted an obviously ethical dimension in the passage
in Chapter 19 where restlessness becomes Rachel's way of overcoming the separateness of jealousy, by regaining the intensities
of sensation and the 'instant':

> Physical movement was the only refuge, in and out of rooms, in
> and out of people's minds, seeking she knew what...But owing
> to the broad sunshine after shaded passages, and to the substance
> of living people after dreams, the group appeared with startling
> intensity, as though the dusty surface had been peeled off
> everything, leaving only the reality and the instant. It had the
> look of a vision printed on the dark at night. White and grey and
> purple figures were scattered on the green, round wicker tables,
> in the middle the flame of the tea-urn made the air waver like a
> faulty sheet of glass, a massive green tree stood over them as if it
> were a moving force held at rest. As she approached she could
> hear Evelyn's voice repeating monotonously, 'Here then—
> here—good doggie, come here'; for a moment nothing seemed
> to happen; it all stood still, and then she realized that one of the

figures was Helen Ambrose; and the dust again began to settle...[41]

Once again, the passage conveys to an extraordinary degree the stages and levels of Rachel's response, as the pure physicality of the surrounding world returns and resolves itself into the terms of her recognition. This is conveyed in the image of the tree, 'as if a moving force held at rest', where the values of movement that animate the text are identified with Rachel's perception, as a response to the world as movement. In Bergson's terms, such movements of image are the basis of our experience, before the world of representable meanings asserts itself and fixes the tree within the speculative grasp of conceptual thought. Bergson's account of perception in *Matter and Memory* argues that our perceptions begin outside ourselves in the pure openness of our body and senses to a world that is then reacted to on the basis of need, habit and memory. Like the ship, the mind is perpetually and at each moment virginal, existing in extensity as the ground of our experience. We exist somewhere before we know where, and before habit and memory contract experience into the foldings of consciousness. Woolf's novel is dedicated to a holding open of this interval. And so the narrative charts the oddity of Rachel's decline into contact with things as her mind dissolves into notations of moving shadows, of noises like animals, of white planks on the deck, patterns of light, blocks of sound, and so on; that she is experiencing time as unaccountable movements of duration that resist the clock and calendar. The presentation of her death, in line with this oddly affirmative logic, offers it as the final release, and as happiness. Indeed Terence responds in this way before he recognizes with full consciousness the truth that he will never see her again. Such a description of dissociation is given also in the narration of Rachel's states of mind during the onset of her illness:

> She supposed...that she was not quite well again. At the same time the wall of her room was painfully white, and curved slightly, instead of being straight and flat. Turning her eyes to the window, she was not reassured by what she saw there. The movement of the blind as it filled with air and blew slowly about, drawing the cord with a little trailing sound along the

floor, seemed to her terrifying, as if it were the movement of an animal in the room...[42]

Rachel kept her eyes fixed upon the peaked shadow on the ceiling, and all her energy was concentrated upon the desire that this shadow should move...

On Thursday morning when Terence went into her room he felt the usual increase of confidence. She turned round and made an effort to remember certain facts from the world that was so many millions of miles away...
      'You say, there they go, rolling off the edge of the hill...'[43]

The sights were all concerned in some plot, some adventure, some escape. The nature of what they were doing changed incessantly, although there was always a reason behind it, which she must endeavour to grasp...[44]

On this day indeed Rachel was conscious of what went on round her. She had come to the surface of the dark, sticky pool, and a wave seemed to bear her up and down with it; she had ceased to have any will of her own; she lay on the top of the wave conscious of some pain, but chiefly of weakness. The wave was replaced by the side of a mountain. her body became a drift of melting snow... Sometimes she could see through the wall in front of her...she pushed her voice out as far as possible, until sometimes it became a bird and flew away, she thought it doubtful whether it ever reached the person she was talking to. There were immense intervals or chasms...her mind...gone flitting round the room...[45]

'I want to know what's going on behind it. I hate these divisions, don't you, Terence?'[46]

This final speech remains the final word in a sense. For Woolf and for Rachel the voyage out is a voyage away from the world of familiar meanings and available, measurable and conventional logic, from the quantitative thinking of science, from the world of Hirst as it were, towards the pure encounter, the activity intrinsic to life in which one is held outside oneself, and in which one experiences duration, the continuity of time in itself. One always returns in the drama of this work to this movement which is precisely no return, but an encounter with the sheer variety of the world. The voyage in the text is one away from England, away from family and friends, towards a purity of an encounter with Terence which preserves itself against any relapse into the commonplace, into indifference or jealousy. At the beginning of Chapter 15, the narrator talks of the ways in which relationships change over time:

> Whether too slight or too vague the ties that bind people casually meeting in a hotel at midnight, they possess one advantage at least over the bonds which unite the elderly... Slight they may be, but vivid and genuine, merely because the power to break them is within the grasp of each, and there is no reason for continuance except a true desire that continue they shall...[47]

Again it is the sense of movement within experience that is compelling here, of encounters which involve people in momentary communications whose condition is freedom, and a kind of provisionality or openness incompatible with mere habit. It is interesting towards the end of the novel that with the realization of love comes the possibility of jealousy, of enclosure. Jealousy had started to emerge as a possibility in the relationship, as in the relationship of Susan and Arthur. Rachel's last words indicate the perverse purity of her attitude: 'Hello, Terence'. It is a speech which never becomes a conversation, which defines their relation as in the last analysis an anticipation that defies language. It is a relation of silences or music more than of words, one existing in the intervals and transitions between speech, and ultimately in the interval between avowal and the marriage vow.

Notes

Introduction

1. Gilles Deleuze and Claire Parnet, *Dialogues* (trans. H. Tomlinson and B. Habberjam; London: Athlone Press, 1987 [1977]), p. 61.

2. Brian Massumi, *A User's Guide to Capitalism and Schizophrenia* (Cambridge, MA: MIT, 1992), pp. 4-5. For a fascinating discussion of the critique of recognition, representation and the model of common sense in the third chapter of *Difference and Repetition*, see Timothy S. Murphy, 'Theatre of Cruelty', in J. Broadhurst (ed.), *Deleuze and the Transcendental Unconscious* (Warwick: *PLI*–Warwick Journal of Philosophy, 1992), pp. 105-35.

3. Cited by Colin Gordon, 'The Subtracting Machine', *I & C* (Spring, 1981), p. 32.

4. Gilles Deleuze, *Nietzsche and Philosophy* (trans. H. Tomlinson; London; Athlone Press, 1983), p. 70.

5. Deleuze and Parnet, *Dialogues*, pp. 95-96.

6. Gordon, 'The Subtracting Machine', p. 32.

7. Deleuze and Parnet, *Dialogues*, p. 49.

8. Deleuze and Parnet, *Dialogues*, pp. 54-55.

9. Deleuze and Parnet, *Dialogues*, p. 40.

10. Deleuze and Parnet, *Dialogues*, p. 40.

11. Thomas Hardy, *Tess of the d'Urbervilles* (London: Dent, 1984), p. 170.

12. Deleuze and Parnet, *Dialogues*, p. 74.

13. Deleuze and Parnet, *Dialogues*, pp. 74-75.

14. Deleuze and Parnet, *Dialogues*, pp. 14-15.

15. Deleuze and Parnet, *Dialogues*, pp. 12-13.

16. Michael Hardt, *Gilles Deleuze: An Apprenticeship in Philosophy* (London: UCL Press, 1993).

Chapter 1: Deleuze And Empiricism

1. Gilles Deleuze, *Proust and Signs* (trans. R. Howard; New York: George Braziller, 1972), p. 161.

2. Deleuze, *Proust and Signs*, p. 166.

3. Murphy, 'Theatre of Cruelty', p. 116.

4. Deleuze, *Proust and Signs*, pp. 129-30.

5.   Marcel Proust, *Remembrance of Things Past* (trans. C.K. Scott Moncrieff and T. Kilmartin; and A. Mayor; London: Penguin Books, 1989), III, p. 899.

6.   Deleuze, *Proust and Signs*, p. 163.

7.   Deleuze, *Proust and Signs*, p. 88.

8.   Proust, *Remembrance of Things Past*, III, p. 925.

9.   Deleuze, *Proust and Signs*, p. 47.

10. Deleuze, *Proust and Signs*, p. 138.

11. Gilles Deleuze, *Empiricism and Subjectivity: An Essay on Hume's Theory of Human Nature* (trans. C.V. Boundas; New York: Columbia University Press, 1991), p. 133.

12. Deleuze, *Empiricism and Subjectivity*, p. 133.

13. Nick Land, 'Machinic Desire', *Textual Practice* 7.3 (1993), p. 472.

14. Land, 'Machinic Desire', p. 472.

15. Brian Massumi, 'Notes on the Translation and Acknowledgements', in Gilles Deleuze and Felix Guattari, *A Thousand Plateaus* (trans. B. Massumi; London: Athlone Press, 1988), p. xvi.

16. Gilles Deleuze and Felix Guattari, *What is Philosophy* (trans. G. Burchell and H. Tomlinson; London: Verso, 1994), p. 24.

17. Ian Buchanan, Review of *What is Philosophy?*, *Textual Practice* 10.1 (1996), p. 222.

18. Deleuze and Guattari, *What is Philosophy?*, p. 207.

19. Deleuze and Guattari, *What is Philosophy?*, p. 65.

20. Deleuze and Guattari, *What is Philosophy?*, p. 16.

21. Gilles Deleuze, *Difference and Repetition* (trans. P. Patton; London: Athlone Press, 1994), p. 1

22. Deleuze, *Difference and Repetition*, p. 69.

23. Deleuze, *Difference and Repetition*, p. 169.

24. Deleuze, *Difference and Repetition*, p. 146.

25. Deleuze, *Difference and Repetition*, p. 165.

26. Deleuze and Parnet, *Dialogues*, p. vii.

27. Deleuze and Guattari, *What is Philosophy?*, p. 2.

28. Deleuze and Parnet, *Dialogues*, p. vii.

29. Deleuze and Parnet, *Dialogues*, p. 24.

30. Buchanan, Review of *What is Philosophy?*, p. 222.

31. Deleuze and Parnet, *Dialogues*, p. 24.

32. In *Difference and Repetition* and *Nietzsche and Philosophy*, Deleuze notes that the Kantian critique was 'equipped to overturn the Image of Thought' (of recognition) (*Difference and Repetition*, p. 136), but that it fell into a reactive compromise with the powers that be, in so far as it fell back upon the conception of thought as the harmonious and prescribed functioning of common sense. These features of Kant's work give Deleuze's readings of Kant an importantly deconstructive flavour, in so far as they uncover within Kant's work necessary but dysfunctional implications, and indicate other potentials within it.

33. See, for instance, the following remarks about the necessity of this

conformity for the possibility of knowledge: 'the relation to a transcendental object, that is the objective reality of our empirical knowledge, rests on the transcendental law, that all appearances, in so far as through them objects are to be given to us, must stand under those *a priori* rules of synthetical unity whereby the interrelating of those appearances in empirical intuition is alone possible. In other words, appearances in experience must stand under the conditions of the necessary unity of apperception...': Immanuel Kant, *Critique of Pure Reason* (trans. N.K. Smith; London: Macmillan, 1970), pp. 137-38.

34. See, for instance, Gilles Deleuze, *The Logic of Sense* (trans. M. Lester with C. Stivale; New York: Columbia University Press, 1990), pp. 105-106.

35. See Deleuze, *The Logic of Sense*, p. 109.

36. Gilles Deleuze, *Bergsonism* (trans. H. Tomlinson and B. Habberjam; New York: Zone, 1991), p. 87.

37. Deleuze, *Difference and Repetition*, p. 140.

38. Deleuze, *Difference and Repetition*, p. 140.

39. Gilles Deleuze, *Spinoza: Practical Philosophy* (trans. R. Hurley; San Francisco: City Lights, 1988), p. 128.

40. Deleuze, *The Logic of Sense*, p. 99.

41. Constantin V. Boundas, 'Deleuze: Serialization and Subject-Formation', in C.V. Boundas and D. Olkowski (eds.), *Gilles Deleuze and the Theatre of Philosophy* (London: Routledge, 1994), p. 104.

42. Deleuze, *Difference and Repetition*, p. 139.

43. Deleuze, *Nietzsche and Philosophy*, p. 40.

44. So as to maintain the continuity of the discussion I have maintained the above distinction between consciousness and mind, even in discussing Deleuze's account of Nietzsche where the terms correspond, more or less, to *ressentiment* and, confusingly, consciousness.

45. Deleuze, *Nietzsche and Philosophy*, p. 114.

46. Alphonso Lingis, *Foreign Bodies* (London: Routledge, 1993), p. 112.

47. Deleuze, *Nietzsche and Philosophy*, p. 125.

48. Deleuze, *Spinoza: Practical Philosophy*, p. 26.

49. Gordon, 'The Subtracting Machine', p. 31.

50. Deleuze, *Spinoza: Practical Philosophy*, p. 127.

51. For a fuller discussion, see *Spinoza: Practical Philosophy*, pp. 127-28.

52. The term is spelt differently as 'haecceity' or 'hecceity' in *A Thousand Plateaus* and *Dialogues*, respectively, and I have conformed to these differences in quotation.

53. Deleuze and Guattari, *A Thousand Plateaus*, p. 261.

54. Deleuze and Parnet, *Dialogues*, p. 92.

55. Deleuze and Parnet, *Dialogues*, p. 92. See also *Spinoza: Practical Philosophy*, pp. 128-30.

56. Deleuze, *Spinoza: Practical Philosophy*, p. 128.

57. Deleuze and Parnet, *Dialogues*, p. 89.

58. Quoted by Gordon, 'The Subtracting Machine', p. 30.

59. Baruch Spinoza, *The Ethics* (trans. S. Shirley; ed. S. Feldman; Indianapolis: Hackett, 1992), II, proposition 23, p. 81.

60. And as the brain corrects the inversion of the visual image on the retina, so also (to take up a Nietzschean idea here) the conscious subject corrects his belatedness by repressing it. But in translation into the terms of consciousness, for reasons discussed above, the creativity of desire becomes lost.

61. Deleuze and Parnet, *Dialogues*, p. viii.

62. See Michael Hardt, *Gilles Deleuze: An Apprenticeship in Philosophy* (London: UCL Press, 1993). The discussion of these paragraphs is much indebted to Hardt's elucidations of Deleuze's ontological thinking, as well as of the scholastic and other, somewhat covert, philosophical contexts for Deleuze's discussions.

63. One of the virtues of Hardt's narrative is to suggest how little in fact his study would lose in terms of its substantial points were it restricted to Deleuze's work on Spinoza alone.

64. Antonio Negri, cover notes to Hardt's book.

65. Deleuze, *Bergsonism*, p. 98.

66. Deleuze, *Bergsonism*, p. 95.

67. Brian Massumi has emphasized the importance of the idea of the virtual in Deleuze's work, as well as its relative neglect by commentators (see Massumi, *A User's Guide to Capitalism and Schizophrenia*, pp. 34-46). Deleuze's uses of the concept of the virtual (and its difference from the concept of possibility) are many. The following paragraph offers a brief account of the temporal ramifications of the concept in line with the discussion here.

The virtual as a term envelops three aspects that define both its multiplicity and its unity. In its purity, the virtual is the real but non-existent repetition of division that is the ultimate resource of the virtual in its second aspect—as a process of active becoming, duration, and in its third aspect—as actualized being. The virtual as the pure form of time subsists as the abyssal and dissociating future-past in the work of the virtual in the, positively ontological, sense of self-differentiating actualization and becoming. The process of becoming, of the unfolding of virtual potential in the actualizing of linear connection and progression, is inscribed always from within by the real but non-actualized repetition of the purely virtual limits of a generative nothingness. To become is self-differentiation, and self-differentiation is a creative process, but it is a creative process that nonetheless presupposes the repetitions of a pure discontinuity that is at once its principle, so to speak, and its fate: a pure virtuality, then, at once non-existent and real inhabits the becoming of the present as its doing and undoing, referring it always to the future and the past. In the explicitly present moment we discern an actualization whose contracted being signifies the processes and forces that it envelops, and the potential it bears within itself.

68. Hardt, *Gilles Deleuze: An Apprenticeship in Philosophy*, p. 14. The quotation from Deleuze is from 'La conception de la difference chez Bergson', *Les études bergsoniennes* 4 (1956), p. 93.

69. See Chapter 3, 'Memory as Virtual Coexistence', in Deleuze, *Bergsonism*, pp. 51-72. The central metaphysical point here is the argument that the past must coexist with the present as the pure condition of its passing. To put it slightly differently, the past is the simultaneous dimension of the unceasing being of the ceasing of the present. This formulation has the advantage at least of suggesting the importance of memory in Bergson's work as our mode of access to the ontologically real but virtual dimension of the past, our psychological participation within duration in the unity of the virtual as a unity of being always constituted as past. Memory repeats the past in recollection within the present divided between passing and the past.

70. Deleuze, *Bergsonism*, p. 103.

71. 'What wills' here because Deleuze is keen to stress that Nietzsche's conception of the agency will cannot be identified with, or reduced to, the volitions of a conscious or moral subject. See Chapter 2 of *Nietzsche and Philosophy*.

72. Deleuze, *Nietzsche and Philosophy*, p. 68. See also here Nietzsche's remarks in *The Genealogy of Morals: An Attack* (trans. F. Goffing; New York: Doubleday, 1956), Preface, pp. iii, 51:

> Was this what my *a priori* demanded of me—that new, immoral, or at any rate non-moral *a priori*—and that mysterious anti-Kantian categorical imperative to which I have hearkened more and more ever since, and not only hearkened...

73. Deleuze, *Nietzsche and Philosophy*, p. 72.

74. Hardt, *Gilles Deleuze: An Apprenticeship in Philosophy*, p. 57.

75. Massumi, *Capitalism and Schizophrenia: A User's Guide*, pp. 107-108.

76. Deleuze and Parnet, *Dialogues*, p. 2.

77. Deleuze and Guattari, *A Thousand Plateaus*, p. 295.

78. Massumi, *Capitalism and Schizophrenia: A User's Guide*, p. 102.

79. Interview with Catherine Clement, *L'Arc* 49 (*Deleuze*), 2nd edn (1980), p. 99.

80. Deleuze and Parnet, *Dialogues*, p. 102.

81. Deleuze and Parnet, *Dialogues*, p. 89.

Chapter 2: Deleuze And Reading

1. Deleuze and Guattari, *What is Philosophy?*, p. 176.

2. Deleuze and Guattari, *A Thousand Plateaus*, p. 4.

3. Walt Whitman, *The Complete Poems* (London: Penguin Books, 1975), p. 302.

4. Deleuze and Parnet, *Dialogues*, p. 96.

5. Deleuze, *Spinoza: Practical Philosophy*, p. 29.

6. Deleuze and Guattari, *A Thousand Plateaus*, p. 261.

7. Deleuze, *Difference and Repetition*, pp. 258-59.

8. Deleuze and Guattari, *A Thousand Plateaus*, p. 314.

9. Deleuze and Parnet, *Dialogues*, p. 120.

10. Deleuze and Parnet, *Dialogues*, p. 121.

11. Deleuze and Guattari, *A Thousand Plateaus*, p. 105.

12. Gilles Deleuze and Felix Guattari, *Kafka* (trans. D. Polan; Minneapolis: University of Minnesota Press, 1986), p. 18.

13. Deleuze and Guattari, *Kafka*, pp. 18-19.

14. Réda Bensmaia, 'On the Concept of Minor Literature', in Boundas and Olkowski (eds.), *Gilles Deleuze and the Theatre of Philosophy*, p. 215.

15. Deleuze and Guattari, *Kafka*, p. 19.

16. Gilles Deleuze, 'He Stuttered', in Boundas and Olkowski (eds.), *Gilles Deleuze and the Theatre of Philosophy*, p. 25.

17. It is as well here to introduce a cautionary note as to the distinction between major and minor literature. There is a kind of rhetorical or polemical aspect in Deleuze and Guattari's formulation which leaves us the possibility of interpreting the terms as concepts which work to maximize our sense of a potential of literature which would still be at work in so called major literature, albeit in ways which such texts would be concerned to suppress. It is striking, certainly, that Deleuze and Guattari never give cases of major literature, to my knowledge, so that we are open to understand minor literature as delineating an intrinsic tendency of all literature. This would accord with the ways mentioned in which Deleuze confronts what could be called the majoritarian in philosophy, as in the work of Kant or Plato, with its minoritarian, deterritorializing elements. As this suggests, the concepts would then work as ways, among other things, of describing modes of reading. Some such caution lies behind my formulations of the differences between the literary texts discussed in this book and the earlier nineteenth-century fictions with which I compare them in passing. Although the term 'minor literature' proves useful at times as a strategic means of distinguishing these writers formally from earlier literary practices, it is not intended that writers such as George Eliot or Charles Dickens be seen as identified with some monolithic and homogeneous fictional practice which would be major.

18. See in particular Chapter 3 of *A Thousand Plateaus*.

19. Deleuze, 'He Stuttered', p. 26.

20. Deleuze, 'He Stuttered', p. 27.

21. Pelagia Goulimari, in her 'On The Line of Flight: How to be a Realist?', *Angelaki* 1.i (1993), pp. 11-27, offers a fascinating reading of these and other aspects of Deleuze and Guattari's book on Kafka, within the context of a discussion of how a thinking of minoritarian becoming can displace the identity thinking which she sees as dominating debates about postmodernism.

22. Deleuze and Guattari, *Kafka*, p. 6.

23. Deleuze and Guattari, *Kafka*, p. 28.

24. Deleuze and Guattari, *Kafka*, pp. 26-27.

25. Paul Patton, 'Anti-Platonism and Art', in Boundas and Olkowski (eds.), *Gilles Deleuze and the Theatre of Philosophy*, p. 155.

26. Patton, 'Anti-Platonism and Art', p. 152.

27. Deleuze, *Difference and Repetition*, p. 67.

28. In *Nietzsche and Philosophy*, Deleuze draws an account of the synthesis of forces as a quantitative inequality which produces reciprocally active and reactive qualities of force. Of these consciousness, as an inherently reactive mode of thought, exceeded and occasioned by the multiple and unconscious working of the body, can only perceive the latter. Sensation, as the perception and affection arising out of the differential intensities produced by forces, remains blind to the genetic productivity of forces from whose encounter the perceived reactive quality derives. In so far as the material is conceived as the given to consciousness, it is also the withheld, the unconscious, since consciousness depends on the accord of the faculties in their relation to the objects of experience. In a memorable phrase from *Difference and Repetition*, p. 140, Deleuze talks of this being as 'not the given but that by which the given is given', not, in the case of sensibility, the empirically imperceptible as such but the imperceptible being of the perceivable. The affect and percept correspond to these unconscious necessities of perception and affection.

29. Deleuze and Guattari, *What is Philosophy?*, p. 176.

30. Deleuze and Guattari, *What is Philosophy?*, p. 173.

31. Deleuze, *Spinoza: Practical Philosophy*, p. 81.

32. Deleuze and Guattari, *What is Philosophy?*, p. 177.

33. Deleuze and Guattari, *What is Philosophy?*, pp. 166-67.

34. Deleuze and Guattari, *What is Philosophy?*, pp. 168-70.

35. Deleuze and Guattari, *What is Philosophy?*, p. 195.

36. Deleuze and Guattari, *A Thousand Plateaus*, p. 76.

37. Deleuze and Guattari, *A Thousand Plateaus*, pp. 80-81.

38. R. Gasché, '*Setzung* and *Übersetzung*: Notes on Paul de Man', in Rajnath (ed.), *Deconstruction: A Critique* (London: Macmillan, 1989), pp. 212-52. See also de Man's own approving reference to this piece in a letter to Wlad Godzich reprinted in a note to Lindsay Waters's introductory essay, in Lindsay Waters (ed.), *Paul de Man, Critical Writings, 1953–1978* (Minneapolis: University of Minnesota Press, 1989), p. lxxiii, or de Man's references to Heidegger in a crucial note to *Allegories of Reading* (New Haven: Yale University Press, 1979), p. 175.

39. Hardt, *Gilles Deleuze: An Apprenticeship in Philosophy*, p. 115.

40. Hardt, *Gilles Deleuze: An Apprenticeship in Philosophy*, pp. xiii-xiv.

41. See *Difference and Repetition*, pp. 64-66.

42. Deleuze and Parnet, *Dialogues*, p. viii.

43. Hardt, *Gilles Deleuze: An Apprenticeship in Philosophy*, p. 18.

44. Deleuze and Guattari, *A Thousand Plateaus*, p. 110.
45. Massumi, *A User's Guide to Capitalism and Schizophrenia*, p. 30.
46. Deleuze and Guattari, *A Thousand Plateaus*, p. 80.
47. Deleuze and Guattari, *A Thousand Plateaus*, p. 109.

Chapter 3: Thomas Hardy—*Jude The Obscure*

1. Friedrich Nietzsche, 'On the Uses and Disadvantages of History for Life' (1874), in *Untimely Meditations* (trans. R.J. Hollingdale; Cambridge: Cambridge University Press, 1983), p. 60.
2. See for instance, John Goode, *Thomas Hardy: The Offensive Truth* (Oxford: Basil Blackwell, 1988); Terry Eagleton, *Criticism and Ideology* (London: Verso, 1978).
3. Thomas Hardy, *Jude the Obscure* (London: Macmillan, 1974), p. 93.
4. Hardy, *Jude the Obscure*, p. 74.
5. Deleuze, *Nietzsche and Philosophy*, p. 71.
6. Deleuze, *Nietzsche and Philosophy*, p. 70.
7. Hardy, *Jude the Obscure*, p. 419.
8. Friedrich Nietzsche, *Thus Spoke Zarathustra* (London: Penguin Books, 1961), Prologue, p. 44.
9. Deleuze and Guattari, *A Thousand Plateaus*, p. 187.
10. Virginia Woolf, 'The Novels of Thomas Hardy', in *Collected Essays* (ed. L. Woolf; London: Hogarth, 1966), I, p. 257.
11. Hardy, *Jude the Obscure*, p. 43.
12. Hardy, *Jude the Obscure*, p. 216.
13. Hardy, *Jude the Obscure*, p. 28.
14. Deleuze, *Nietzsche and Philosophy*, p. 70.
15. Deleuze, *Nietzsche and Philosophy*, p. 70.
16. Deleuze, *Nietzsche and Philosophy*, p. 70.
17. *The Genealogy of Morals*, II, i, pp. 189-90.
18. See Chapter 1 for a fuller discussion of some of these issues.
19. Deleuze, *Nietzsche and Philosophy*, p. 70.
20. Gilles Deleuze, 'The Selective Test' (from *Difference and Repetition*), reprinted in C.V. Boundas (ed.), *The Deleuze Reader* (New York: Columbia University Press, 1993), p. 86.
21. Deleuze, 'The Selective Test', p. 89.
22. Jean-François Lyotard, 'Answer to the Question: What is the Postmodern?', in *The Postmodern Explained to Children, Correspondence 1982–1985* (trans. J. Pefanis and M. Thomas; London: Turnaround, 1992), p. 22.
23. Lyotard, 'Answer to the Question: What is the Postmodern?', p. 24.
24. Hardy, *Jude the Obscure*, p. 30.
25. Hardy, *Jude the Obscure*, p. 31.
26. Hardy, *Jude the Obscure*, p. 38.
27. Deleuze, 'The Selective Test', p. 86.

28. John Bayley, *An Essay on Hardy* (Cambridge: Cambridge University Press, 1978), p. 199.

29. Hardy, *Jude the Obscure*, p. 23.

30. Hardy, *Jude the Obscure*, p. 26.

31. Letter to Edmund Gosse, 10 November, 1895, in R.L. Purdy and M. Millgate (eds.), *The Collected Letters of Thomas Hardy* (Oxford: Clarendon Press, 1980), II, p. 93.

32. Hardy, *Letters*, II, p. 93.

33. Bayley, *An Essay on Hardy*, p. 196.

34. Hardy, *Jude the Obscure*, p. 120.

35. Hardy, *Jude the Obscure*, p. 120.

36. Hardy, *Jude the Obscure*, p. 44.

37. Hardy, *Jude the Obscure*, p. 302.

38. Hardy, *Jude the Obscure*, pp. 395-96.

39. Hardy, *Jude the Obscure*, p. 419.

40. Gilles Deleuze, *Cinema I: The Movement-Image* (trans. H. Tomlinson and B. Habberjam; London: Athlone Press, 1992), p. 17.

41. Such an emphasis on the disjunctive synthesis has been mentioned above in relation to Deleuze's readings of Nietzsche, but it is a recurrent though varying strain within his work. In *Difference and Repetition* it receives perhaps its most systematic elucidation as the synthesis of the pure form of time, which creates the differential repetition of the future—the time of experiment, of learning and thought—as it achieves a violent loosening of what has been, of precept, recognition and the exemplarity of the concept. In *Difference and Repetition*, moreover, Deleuze conceives of this displacement in terms productive for the study of literature, in terms of the concept of the 'caesura'. But other references could equally be given.

42. Constantin V. Boundas, 'Introduction', *The Deleuze Reader*, p. 15.

43. Boundas, 'Introduction', *The Deleuze Reader*, p. 21.

44. Deleuze, *Cinema I: The Movement-Image*, p. 17.

Chapter 4: George Gissing—*The Odd Women*

1. Virginia Woolf, 'George Gissing', in *Collected Essays* (ed. L. Woolf; London: Hogarth, 1966), I, p. 297.

2. Woolf, 'George Gissing', p. 299.

3. John Goode, *George Gissing: Ideology and Fiction* (London: Vision, 1978), p. 147.

4. Goode, *George Gissing: Ideology and Fiction*, p. 147.

5. Jacob Korg, *George Gissing: A Critical Biography* (Brighton: Harvester Press, 1980), p. 5.

6. David Gryllis, *The Paradox of Gissing* (London: Allen & Unwin, 1986), p. xi.

7. Alice B. Markow, 'George Gissing: Advocate or Provocateur of the Women's Movement?', *English Literature in Transition* 25.2 (1985), p. 58.

8.   George Gissing, *Charles Dickens: A Critical Study* (London: Gresham, 1903), p. 156.

9.   George Gissing, *The Letters of George Gissing to Edward Bertz, 1887–1903* (ed. A.C. Young; New Brunswick, NJ: Rutgers University Press, 1961), p. 171.

10.   George Gissing, *The Odd Women* (London: Virago, 1980), p. 167.

11.   Deleuze and Guattari, *What is Philosophy?*, p. 174.

12.   Deleuze and Guattari, *What is Philosophy?*, p. 175.

13.   Entitled '*Authentic* Ressentiment: *Generic Discontinuities and Ideologemes in the "Experimental" Novels of George Gissing*', Jameson's discussion traces a development in Gissing's treatment of the narrative and political complexities of *ressentiment* from the early work, such as *Demos* and *The Nether World*, to the fictions of the 1890s. Jameson's discussion of the earlier novels had demonstrated how in *Demos*, for instance, the ascription of *ressentiment* to the militant working-class characters also inevitably rebounded on the narrator, and seemed in its factitiousness to carry an inner reproach to those of the upper class whose attitudes he sought to appropriate:

> What is most striking about the theory of *ressentiment* is its unavoidably autoreferential structure. In *Demos*, certainly, the conclusion is inescapable: Gissing resents Richard, and what he resents most is the latter's *ressentiment*...[and of the motivation behind the narrator's assumption of upper class attitudes] far from being only that of an identification with the attitudes of the upper classes, is also, given the system of Gissing's own ambivalence, a conduct of *ressentiment* against them, tending to embarrass and to compromise even those on whose behalf it seemed to testify (*The Political Unconscious* [London: Methuen, 1981], p. 202).

Jameson identifies in the Gissing of *The Odd Women* and *New Grub Street*, however, an absence of any such discernible attitude, and he comments on what he terms the 'electrical dryness' of their style, and the 'secret intensity' of the 'deliberately unexpressed' strong feelings and 'affective silences' which mark out a language now radically depersonalized as a kind of self-mutilation of the desires and aspirations which would correspond to narrative *ressentiment*. In this way, *ressentiment* is said to be negated, and become 'authentic'. There are some important differences also here, most particularly with Jameson's claim that *ressentiment* becomes converted into an authentic political attitude of resistance in Gissing's later fiction, because it is involved with a radical suspension of the desires that had surfaced in the more inauthentic class attitudinizing evident in narrative elements in the earlier work. This chapter traces ethical and psychological features of *ressentiment* in this novel, while also contesting somewhat Jameson's vindication of a politically redeemed attitude of *ressentiment* that extends to its own operative desires.

14.   Deleuze, *Nietzsche and Philosophy*, p. 115.

15.   See Korg, *George Gissing: A Critical Biography*, p. 7.

16.   Gissing, *The Odd Women*, p. 6.

17. Gissing, *The Odd Women*, p. 5.

18. Gissing, *The Odd Women*, p. 2.

19. Gissing, *The Odd Women*, p. 2.

20. Gissing, *The Odd Women*, p. 37.

21. Gissing, *The Odd Women*, p. 56.

22. Gissing, *The Odd Women*, p. 35.

23. See, for instance, Deleuze and Guattari, *What is Philosophy?*, pp. 18-19.

24. The Other Person is the condition by which my experience can be organized as one possible experience of the world, and distinguished from its perceptual objects. In *The Logic of Sense*, this is summarized succinctly in the course of a discussion of Tournier's rewriting of *Robinson Crusoe*:

> In fact, perceptual laws affecting the constitution of objects (form-background, etc.), the temporal determination of the subject, and the successive development of worlds, seemed to us to depend on the possible as the structure-Other. Even desire, whether it be desire for the object or desire for Others, depends on this structure. I desire an object only as expressed by the Other in the mode of the possible; I desire in the Other only the possible worlds the Other expresses. The Other appears as the element which organizes elements into earth, and earth into bodies, bodies into objects, and which regulates and measures object, perception, and desire all at once . . . (*The Logic of Sense*, p. 318).

25. It is on such features that Nietzsche's account in *The Genealogy of Morals* depends for the transmutation of *ressentiment*.

26. This discussion touches on relevant aspects of Deleuze's discussion of the sad passions in his work on Spinoza, where the task of ethics emerges as in a large part the task of elucidating the insistent repetitions of the unconscious emotions, the sad passions which testify to the still operative constraints of past relations. The depth, range, subtlety, power and cogency of Spinoza's analysis in the *Ethics* makes his text the most invaluable reference here.

27. Deleuze, *Proust and Signs*, p. 9.

28. Gissing, *The Odd Women*, p. 148.

29. Gissing, *The Odd Women*, p. 38.

30. Gissing, *The Odd Women*, p. 17.

31. Gissing, *The Odd Women*, p. 43.

32. Gissing, *The Odd Women*, pp. 278-79.

33. Gilles Deleuze, 'Coldness and Cruelty', in *Masochism* (trans. J. McNeill; New York: Zone, 1989), p. 115.

34. Deleuze, 'Coldness and Cruelty', p. 110.

35. Deleuze, 'Coldness and Cruelty', p. 125.

36. Deleuze, 'Coldness and Cruelty', p. 19.

37. Nicholas Blincoe, 'Deleuze and Masochism', in Broadhurst (ed), *Deleuze and the Transcendental Unconscious*, pp. 81-96.

38. Gryllis, *The Paradox of George Gissing*, p. 149.

39. Gryllis, *The Paradox of George Gissing*, p. 168.

Chapter 5: Joseph Conrad—*The Shadow-Line*

1. Joseph Conrad, *The Shadow-Line* (London: Penguin Books, 1986), p. 39.
2. Conrad, *The Shadow-Line*, p. 39.
3. Conrad, *The Shadow-Line*, p. 40.
4. Conrad, *The Shadow-Line*, p. 144.
5. Conrad, *The Shadow-Line*, p. 92.
6. Deleuze and Parnet, *Dialogues*, p. 59.
7. Deleuze and Parnet, *Dialogues*, p. 65.
8. Conrad, *The Shadow-Line*, p. 120.
9. Deleuze and Parnet, *Dialogues*, p. 52.
10. Deleuze and Parnet, *Dialogues*, p. 64.
11. The ways in which in Conrad's writing a kind of sensory intensity combines with a disruption of narrative and stylistic continuity is, for Fredric Jameson, an indication of 'the ambivalent value of Conrad's impressionism' (*The Political Unconscious*, p. 237), its ambivalence a matter of its symbolic, and culturally opportune, resolution of the conflict, broadly, of 'romance and reification'. The discussion of this chapter benefits from Jameson's discussion, though it sees in what Jameson sees as the romantic, utopian dimension of Conrad's 'sensorium', the various means of a Deleuzian 'line of flight'. Here material encounters elicit kinds of transformation, so that sensation becomes, in the world of the novel, a stimulus to new thoughts and departures. These exceed the logic of will merely, as, in expression, the event of writing through its rhetorical and rhythmic features evokes new groupings. For Jameson, Conrad's writing finds its limit and power in an aesthetic which ultimately derealizes the object, heightening and intensifying sight and hearing into semi-autonomous domains of experience, and thus compensating for a cultural reification and fragmentation of the image, while abetting it.
12. Conrad, *The Shadow-Line*, p. 131.
13. Conrad, *The Shadow-Line*, p. 113.
14. Conrad, *The Shadow-Line*, pp. 43-44.
15. Conrad, *The Shadow-Line*, p. 63.
16. Conrad, *The Shadow-Line*, p. 60.
17. Conrad, *The Shadow-Line*, p. 45.
18. Conrad, *The Shadow-Line*, p. 55.
19. Conrad, *The Shadow-Line*, p. 90.
20. Conrad, *The Shadow-Line*, p. 68.
21. Deleuze, *Spinoza: Practical Philosophy*, p. 21.
22. Conrad, *The Shadow-Line*, p. 57.
23. Deleuze, *Spinoza: Practical Philosophy*, p. 59.
24. Deleuze, *Spinoza: Practical Philosophy*, p. 73. The links with Nietzschean *ressentiment* are obvious here.

25. Deleuze, *Spinoza: Practical Philosophy*, p. 57.

26. Conrad, *The Shadow-Line*, p. 39.

27. Conrad, *The Shadow-Line*, p. 48.

28. Conrad, *The Shadow-Line*, p. 53.

29. Conrad, *The Shadow-Line*, p. 78.

30. Deleuze, *The Logic of Sense*, p. 149.

31. Deleuze, *The Logic of Sense*, p. 166.

32. Deleuze and Parnet, *Dialogues*, p. 65.

33. In *The Logic of Sense*, Deleuze writes of the necessarily reciprocal relation between language and the event. In the first place, this is because the event depends on language for its expression, since language has potentials beyond its representative functions. In the second place, it is because, accordingly, language depends on events, since it participates as metaphysical sense in the incorporeal effects of a surface which is distinguishable from the physical order of causes, in so far as these pertain to corporeal features and actualizations, including those of language itself.

34. Deleuze and Parnet, *Dialogues*, p. 65.

35. Conrad, *The Shadow-Line*, p. 126.

36. Conrad, *The Shadow-Line*, p. 116.

37. Conrad, *The Shadow-Line*, p. 143.

38. Deleuze, *The Logic of Sense*, p. 151.

39. Conrad, *The Shadow-Line*, pp. 72-73.

Chapter 6: Virginia Woolf—*The Voyage Out*

1. Sue Roe, *Writing and Gender: Virginia Woolf's Writing Practice* (London: Harvester, 1990), p. 3.

2. Clare Hanson, *Virginia Woolf* (London: Macmillan, 1994), p. 34.

3. Quentin Bell, *Virginia Woolf: A Biography* (London: Triad/Paladin, 1976), p. 125.

4. Virginia Woolf, 'A Sketch of the Past', in *Moments of Being* (ed. J. Schulkind; London: Sussex University Press, 1976), p. 72.

5. Harvena Richter, *Virginia Woolf: The Inward Voyage* (Princeton, NJ: Princeton University Press, 1970), p. 40.

6. Richter, *Virginia Woolf*, p. 38.

7. Henri Bergson, *Creative Evolution* (trans. A. Mitchell; London: Macmillan, 1964), p. 319.

8. Richter, *Virginia Woolf*, p. 39.

9. Deleuze, *Cinema I: The Movement-Image*, p. 9. Quotation from Bergson from *Creative Evolution*, p. 322.

10. Deleuze, *Cinema I: The Movement-Image*, p. 11.

11. Deleuze and Guattari, *A Thousand Plateaus*, p. 281.

12. Deleuze and Guattari, *A Thousand Plateaus*, p. 281.

13. See Henri Bergson, *The Two Sources of Morality and Religion* (trans. R.A. Audra and C. Brereton with the assistance of W.H. Carter; Notre

Dame, IN: University of Notre Dame Press, 1986), pp. 195-96.

14. Deleuze, *Bergsonism*, p. 112.

15. Deleuze and Guattari, *A Thousand Plateaus*, pp. 281-82.

16. Deleuze, *Bergsonism*, p. 105. The quotation from Bergson is from *Creative Evolution*, p. 43.

17. Virginia Woolf, *The Voyage Out* (London: Granada, 1978), p. 9.

18. Woolf, *The Voyage Out*, p. 41.

19. Woolf, *The Voyage Out*, p. 78.

20. Woolf, *The Voyage Out*, p. 86.

21. Woolf, *The Voyage Out*, p. 40.

22. Woolf, *The Voyage Out*, p. 130.

23. Woolf, *The Voyage Out*, p. 122.

24. Woolf, *The Voyage Out*, p. 200.

25. Woolf, *The Voyage Out*, p. 144.

26. Woolf, *The Voyage Out*, p. 59.

27. Bergson, *Creative Evolution*, p. 187.

28. Deleuze, *Bergsonism*, pp. 110-11. The quotations from Bergson are from *The Two Sources of Morality and Religion*, p. 254 and p. 40.

29. See *The Two Sources of Morality and Religion*, pp. 195-96.

30. Woolf, *The Voyage Out*, pp. 174-75.

31. Woolf, *The Voyage Out*, p. 175.

32. Woolf, *The Voyage Out*, p. 13.

33. Woolf, *The Voyage Out*, p. 187.

34. Woolf, *The Voyage Out*, pp. 337-38.

35. Woolf, *The Voyage Out*, p. 363.

36. Woolf, *The Voyage Out*, p. 331.

37. Woolf, *The Voyage Out*, p. 11.

38. Woolf, *The Voyage Out*, p. 35.

39. I have mentioned the discussions of Clare Hanson and Sue Roe as bearing on this.

40. Woolf, *The Voyage Out*, p. 146.

41. Woolf, *The Voyage Out*, p. 311.

42. Woolf, *The Voyage Out*, p. 392.

43. Woolf, *The Voyage Out*, p. 398.

44. Woolf, *The Voyage Out*, p. 408.

45. Woolf, *The Voyage Out*, pp. 414-15.

46. Woolf, *The Voyage Out*, p. 361.

47. Woolf, *The Voyage Out*, p. 228.

Bibliography

1. Primary Works

By Deleuze

Bergsonism (trans. H. Tomlinson and B. Habberjam; New York: Zone, 1988 [1966]).

Cinema I: The Movement-Image (trans. H. Tomlinson and B. Habberjam; London: Athlone Press, 1986 [1983]).

Cinema II: The Time-Image (trans. H. Tomlinson and R. Galeta; London: Athlone Press, 1989 [1985]).

'Coldness and Cruelty', in *Masochism* (trans. J. McNeill; New York: Zone, 1989 [1967]), pp. 7-138.

The Deleuze Reader (ed. C.V. Boundas; New York: Columbia University Press, 1993).

Dialogues (with Claire Parnet) (trans. H. Tomlinson and B. Habberjam; London: Athlone Press, 1987 [1977]).

Empiricism and Subjectivity (trans. C.V. Boundas; New York: Columbia University Press, 1991 [1953]).

Expressionism in Philosophy: Spinoza (trans. M. Joughin; New York: Zone, 1992 [1968]).

The Fold: Leibniz and the Baroque (trans. T. Conley; London: Athlone Press, 1993 [1988]).

Foucault (trans. S. Hand; Minneapolis: University of Minnesota Press, 1986 [1986]).

'He Stuttered', in *Gilles Deleuze and the Theatre of Philosophy* (ed. C.V. Boundas and D. Olkowski; London: Routledge, 1994), pp. 23-29.

Kant's Critical Philosophy (trans. H. Tomlinson and B. Habberjam; London: Athlone Press, 1984 [1963]).

The Logic of Sense (trans. M. Lester with C. Stivale; London: Athlone Press, 1990 [1969]).

Nietzsche and Philosophy (trans. H. Tomlinson; London: Athlone Press, 1983 [1962]).

Proust and Signs (trans. R. Howard; New York: George Braziller, 1972 [1964]).

Spinoza: Practical Philosophy (trans. R. Hurley; San Francisco: City Lights, 1988 [1970]).

By Deleuze and Guattari

A Thousand Plateaus (trans. B. Massumi; London: Athlone Press, 1988 [1980]).

Kafka: Towards a Minor Literature (trans. D. Polan; Minneapolis: University of Minnesota Press, 1986 [1975]).

Anti-Oedipus (trans. R. Hurley, M. Seem, and H.R. Lane; Minneapolis: University of Minnesota Press, 1987 [1972]).

What is Philosophy? (trans. H. Tomlinson and G. Burchell; New York: Columbia University Press, 1994 [1991]).

2. Secondary Works

Austin, J.L. *How to Do Things with Words* (Oxford: Oxford University Press, 1976).

Bayley, J., *An Essay on Hardy* (Cambridge: Cambridge University Press, 1978).

Bell, Q., *Virginia Woolf: A Biography* (London: Triad/Paladin, 1976).

Bensmaia, R., 'On the Concept of Minor Literature', in Boundas and Olkowski (eds.), *Gilles Deleuze and the Theatre of Philosophy*, pp. 213-28.

Bergson, H., *Creative Evolution* (trans. A. Mitchell; London: Macmillan, 1964 [1907]).

—*Matter and Memory* (trans. N.M. Paul and W.S. Palmer; New York: Zone, 1991 [1908]).

—*The Two Sources of Morality and Religion* (trans. R.A. Audra and C. Brereton with the assistance of W.H. Carter; Notre Dame, IN: University of Notre Dame Press, 1986 [1932]).

Blincoe, N., 'Deleuze and Masochism', in Broadhurst (ed.), *Deleuze and the Transcendental Unconscious*, pp. 81-96.

Bogue, R., *Deleuze and Guattari* (London: Routledge, 1989).

—'Gilles Deleuze: The Aesthetics of Force', in Patton (ed.), *Deleuze*, pp. 257-69.

Boundas, C.V., 'Deleuze: Serialization and Subject-Formation', in Boundas and Olkowski (eds.), *Gilles Deleuze and the Theatre of Philosophy*, pp. 99-116.

—'Deleuze-Bergson: An Ontology of the Virtual', in Patton (ed.), *Deleuze*, pp. 81-106.

Boundas, C.V., and D. Olkowski (eds.), *Gilles Deleuze and the Theatre of Philosophy* (London: Routledge, 1994).

Broadhurst, J. (ed.), *Deleuze and the Transcendental Unconscious* (*PLI*–Warwick Journal of Philosophy, 1992).

Buchanan, I., Review of *What is Philosophy?*, *Textual Practice* 10.1 (1996), pp. 217-22.

Conrad, J., *The Shadow-Line* (London: Penguin Books, 1986 [1917]).

de Man, P., *Allegories of Reading* (New Haven: Yale University Press, 1979).

—*The Resistance to Theory* (Minneapolis: University of Minnesota Press, 1986).

Eagleton, T., *Criticism and Ideology* (London: Verso, 1978).

Ebbatson, R., *Thomas Hardy: The Margin of the Unexpressed* (Sheffield: Sheffield Academic Press, 1993).

Foucault, M., 'Theatrum Philosophicum', in M. Foucault, *Language, Counter-Memory, Practice* (trans. D.F. Bouchard and S. Simon; Ithaca, NY: Cornell University Press, 1977), p. 191.

Freud, S., 'Beyond the Pleasure Principle', in *Penguin Freud Library*, XI (trans. J. Strackey; London: Penguin, 1991 [1920]), pp. 271-338.

Gasché, R., '*Setzung* and *Übersetzung*: Notes on Paul de Man', in *Deconstruction: A Critique* (ed. Rajnath; London: Macmillan, 1989), pp. 212-52.

Gissing, G., *The Odd Women* (London: Virago, 1980 [1893]).

—*The Letters of George Gissing to Edward Bertz, 1887–1903* (ed. A.C. Young; New Brunswick, NJ: Rutgers University Press, 1961).

—*Charles Dickens: A Critical Study* (London: Gresham, 1903 [1896]).

Goode, J., *George Gissing: Ideology and Fiction* (London: Vision, 1978).

—*Thomas Hardy: The Offensive Truth* (Oxford: Basil Blackwell, 1988).

Gordon, C., 'The Subtracting Machine', *I & C* (Spring 1981), pp. 27-40.

Goulimari, P., 'On The Line of Flight: How to be a Realist?', *Angelaki* 1.i (1993), pp. 11-27.

Gryllis, D., *The Paradox of Gissing* (London: Allen & Unwin, 1986).

Hanson, C., *Virginia Woolf* (London: Macmillan, 1994).

Hardt, M., *Gilles Deleuze: An Apprenticeship in Philosophy* (London: UCL, 1993).

Hardy, T., *Tess of the d'Urbervilles* (London: Dent, 1984 [1891]).

—*Jude the Obscure* (London: Macmillan, 1974 [1896]).

—*The Collected Letters of Thomas Hardy*, II (ed. R.L. Purdy and M. Millgate; Oxford: Clarendon Press, 1980).

Jameson, F., *The Political Unconscious* (London: Methuen, 1981).

Kant, I., *Critique of Pure Reason* (trans. N.K. Smith; London: Macmillan, 1970 [1787]).

Klossowski, P., *Sade My Neighbour* (trans. A. Lingis; London: Quartet Books, 1992 [1947]).

Korg, J., *George Gissing: A Critical Biography* (Brighton: Harvester, 1980).

Land, N., 'Machinic Desire', *Textual Practice* 7.3 (1993), pp. 471-82.

Lingis, A., *Foreign Bodies* (London: Routledge, 1993).

Lyotard, J.-F., 'Answer to the Question: What is the Postmodern?', in *The Postmodern Explained to Children, Correspondence 1982–1985* (trans. J. Pefanis and M. Thomas; London: Turnaround, 1992 [1986]).

Macherey, P., 'The Encounter with Spinoza', in Patton (ed.), *Deleuze*, pp. 139-61.

Markow, A.B., 'George Gissing: Advocate or Provocateur of the Women's Movement?', *English Literature in Transition* 25.2 (1985), pp. 58-73.

Murphy, T.S. 'Theatre of Cruelty', in Broadhurst (ed.), *Deleuze and the Transcendental Unconscious*, pp. 105-35.

Massumi, B., *A User's Guide to Capitalism and Schizophrenia* (Cambridge, MA: MIT, 1992).

Nietzsche, F., *Untimely Meditations* (trans. R.J. Hollingdale; Cambridge: Cambridge University Press, 1983 [1893]).

—*Thus Spoke Zarathustra* (London: Penguin Books, 1961 [1883–85]).

—*The Genealogy of Morals: An Attack* (trans. F. Goffing; New York: Doubleday, 1956 [1887]).

Patton, P., 'Notes for a Glossary', *I & C* (Spring 1981), pp. 41-48.

—'Anti-Platonism and Art', in Boundas and Olkowski (eds.), *Gilles Deleuze and the Theatre of Philosophy*, pp. 141-56.

Patton, P. (ed.), *Deleuze: A Critical Reader* (Oxford: Blackwell, 1996).

Proust, M., *Remembrance of Things Past* (3 vols.; trans. C.K. Scott Moncrieff and T. Kilmartin; and by A. Mayor; London: Penguin Books, 1989 [1913–27]).

Readings, B., *Introducing Lyotard* (London: Routledge, 1991).

Richter, H., *Virginia Woolf: The Inward Voyage* (Princeton, NJ: Princeton University Press, 1970).

Roe, S., *Writing and Gender: Virginia Woolf's Writing Practice* (London: Harvester, 1990).

Smith, D.W., 'Deleuze's Theory of Sensation: Overcoming the Kantian Duality', in Patton (ed.), *Deleuze*, pp. 29-56.

Spinoza, B., *The Ethics* (trans. S. Shirley; ed. S. Feldman; Indianapolis: Hackett, 1992).

Waters, L. (ed.), *Paul de Man, Critical Writings, 1953–1978* (Minneapolis: University of Minnesota Press, 1989).

Whitman, W., *The Complete Poems* (London: Penguin Books, 1975).

Woolf, V., *The Voyage Out* (London: Granada, 1978 [1915]).

—'A Sketch of the Past', in *Moments of Being* (ed. J. Schulkind; London: Sussex University Press, 1976), pp. 61-137.

—'George Gissing', in *Collected Essays* (ed. L. Woolf; London: Hogarth, 1966), I, pp. 297-301.

—'The Novels of Thomas Hardy', in *Collected Essays* (ed. L. Woolf; London: Hogarth, 1966), I, pp. 256-66.

Author Index